#LANGUAGE HACKING

A CONVERSATION COURSE
FOR BEGINNERS

MANDARIN

> ### Learn how to speak Mandarin
> ### – from day one!

BENNY LEWIS
AND
DR. LICHENG GU

First published in Great Britain by Teach Yourself in 2021
An imprint of John Murray Press
A division of Hodder and Stoughton Ltd.
An Hachette UK company.
Copyright © Brendan Lewis 2021
The right of Brendan (Benny) Lewis to be identified as the Author of the Work has been
asserted by him in accordance with the Copyright, Designs and Patents Act 1988.
Database right Hodder & Stoughton (makers).
Co-Author Dr. Licheng Gu
Cover image © Allison Hooban
Illustrations © Will McPhail
The Teach Yourself name is a registered trademark of Hachette UK.

A CIP catalogue record for this title is available from the British Library.

Library of Congress Catalog Card Number: on file.
Paperback ISBN 9781473674271
eBook ISBN 9781473674295
Amazon eBook ISBN 9781473674288

Typeset by Integra
Printed and bound by CPI Group (UK) Ltd, Croydon CR0 4YY

John Murray Press policy is to use papers that are natural, renewable and recyclable
products and made from wood grown in sustainable forests. The logging and
manufacturing processes are expected to conform to the environmental regulations of the
country of origin.

Carmelite House
50 Victoria Embankment
London EC4Y 0DZ

www.teachyourself.com

Nicholas Brealey Publishing
Hachette Book Group
Market Place, Center 53, State Street
Boston, MA 02109, USA

Also available
in ebook

YOUR MISSIONS

UNIT 1: TALKING ABOUT ME

UNIT 2: ASKING ABOUT YOU

UNIT 3: I LIKE SPEAKING MANDARIN

A NOTE FROM BENNY

It's true that some people spend years studying Mandarin Chinese before they finally get around to speaking the language.

But I have a better idea. Let's skip the years of studying and jump right to the speaking part.

Sound crazy? No, it's language hacking.

#LanguageHacking is a completely different approach to learning a new language. It's not magic. It's not something only 'other people' can do. It's simply about being smart with how you learn: learning what's indispensable, skipping what's not and using what you've learned to have real conversations in Mandarin right away. As a language hacker, I find shortcuts to learning new languages – tricks and techniques to crack the language code and make learning simple so I can get fluent faster. When it comes to learning new languages, I focus on getting the biggest bang for my buck.

There's no need to learn every word and grammar rule before you start using the language. You just need to know the most common and the most versatile phrases you'll need in most situations, and how to 'speak around' the problem when there's something you don't understand or know how to say yet.

#LanguageHacking isn't just a course. It's a new way of thinking about language learning. It shows you how to learn a language as well as giving you all the language you need – and none of what you don't. You can use it on your own or with any other book to start speaking languages faster.

I'd like to show you how it's done. See you on the inside.

Benny

Benny Lewis, Language Hacker

AUTHOR BIOGRAPHIES

Irish native Benny Lewis speaks over ten languages – all self-taught. In 2003, he spoke only one language: English. After university, he moved to Spain and was soon frustrated that he could not speak Spanish after six months of studying. So he decided to abandon traditional learning approaches and just start speaking – and everything changed. Today Benny is known as The Irish Polyglot and speaks Mandarin Chinese, Arabic, French, German, Spanish, Italian, Irish Portuguese, Hungarian and American Sign Language. He is the author of the bestselling book, *Fluent in 3 months* and also runs www.fluentin3months.com, where

he breaks down the language learning process for busy people. Lewis is a full-time 'language hacker', and devotes his time to finding better, faster, and more efficient ways to learn languages.

Dr. Licheng Gu 顾利程 is a professor of Chinese language instruction and the East Asia Liaison in the Office of the Vice President for International Relations at Northwestern University. Besides numerous articles and book chapters, Professor Gu has published three books in the field of teaching Chinese as a foreign language: *Picture Characters: Learning Chinese through Pictographs, Learning Chinese with Lulu and Maomao* and *An Analysis of Chinese Teaching in American Universities: Its Past, Present, and Future.* He is highly recognized in Chinese language teacher training at home and abroad and serves as Visiting Professor at Beijing Language and Culture University.

HOW TO USE THIS COURSE

#LanguageHacking isn't like traditional courses. It's a conversation course, which means you will focus on building the language skills you need to have meaningful, real-life conversations with other people in Mandarin – right away. By the end of this course, you'll be able to introduce yourself and ask and answer hundreds of typical questions in Mandarin. You'll know how to find and connect with other Mandarin speakers no matter where you live. And you will gain the skills and strategies to have countless conversations entirely in Mandarin – as well as the confidence to keep them going.

#LanguageHacking can be used either on its own or alongside any other language course – whether it's a book, app, online, audio or in the classroom. Just grab your notebook and get started!

WHAT YOU'LL FIND INSIDE

This course will challenge you to speak from day one by completing ten speaking missions, which will grow your conversational abilities in Mandarin. Each of the features explained below are designed to prepare you for your missions. You can complete the missions on your own, but you'll progress much faster if you use the language with real people, so, if you don't have a study buddy, I encourage you to submit your missions to the #LanguageHacking community for practice and feedback.

SPEAKING FROM DAY 1

You can't learn to play the piano until you sit down and put your fingers on the keys. You can't play tennis until you pick up the racket. And you can't learn a language if you don't speak it. By speaking from day one, you will:

- pick up expressions and language from others
- notice the expression gaps in your language you need to fill
- become aware of how other people say things
- get feedback from others
- improve your pronunciation and fluency
- conquer the fear of speaking a new language
- feel motivated by hearing your own progress.

BUILD YOUR LANGUAGE SKILLS

Build language through typical conversations

Each unit takes you through two conversations in Mandarin that show you how the language is used in common, everyday contexts. The conversations build on each other to grow your vocabulary and prepare you for your mission. Treat each conversation like a lesson, and make sure you understand everything before you move on to the next conversation.

Figure it out exercises

You'll read each conversation and listen to the audio, then I'll help you **Figure it Out**. These exercises train you to start understanding Mandarin on your own – through context, recognizing patterns and applying other language learning strategies – without relying on translations. By figuring out language for yourself, you'll internalize it better and recall it faster when you need it.

Notice exercises

Every conversation is followed by a phrase list with the key phrases, expressions and vocab to know from that conversation, with English translations and pronunciation to help you. **Notice** exercises get you thinking about the new language and noticing how the language works, so you're gaining an intuitive understanding of Mandarin.

Practice exercises

Practice exercises reinforce what you learn. You'll piece together different parts of what you know to figure out how to create new Mandarin phrases on your own.

Put it together

Finally, you'll take everything you've learned and **Put it Together** to create your own repertoire in Mandarin. I'll help you prepare 'me-specific' language you can use in real-life conversations that's actually relevant to you.

SUPPORT, TECHNIQUES AND STRATEGIES

In *Language Hacking*, your ability to have conversations in Mandarin is not limited by the number of words you know.

#LanguageHacks

You'll learn unconventional shortcuts to boost your language abilities exponentially. I reveal the different patterns, rules and tools to help you crack the code and get fluent faster. Each of the ten hacks equips you with techniques you can use in this course and throughout the rest of your learning journey.

Conversation strategies

You'll learn essential conversation strategies, like conversation connectors, filler words, and survival phrases to strike up conversations and keep them flowing.

Grammar & pronunciation

We'll cover the foundation of the grammar you need to know, but I won't overload you with what's not essential to communication. I'll help you understand the important parts of Chinese pronunciation and share techniques to help you get them right.

I'll share more insights as we go along – like culture tips about Mandarin speakers and Mandarin-speaking countries, vocab tips on how to get creative with new phrases, and mini-hacks for better learning.

Progress you can see

You will see your progress build steadily throughout this course. Before you finish each unit, you'll check your understanding with audio practice that acts as a 'virtual conversation partner'. This practice gives you time to collect your thoughts and speak at your own pace. Before you move on to your mission, you'll do a self-assessment checklist to make sure you're prepared and to keep a visual record of the progress you're making.

MISSIONS

Each unit ends with three tasks that you'll complete as your final mission.

STEP 1: build your script

To get ready for spoken practice with other people, you'll build 'me specific' scripts with the language you need to talk about your life. These scripts make sure you're learning useful Mandarin phrases that are truly relevant to you.

STEP 2: speak Mandarin with other people

Speaking from day one is the best way I've found to quickly reach fluency. I'll help you implement this strategy, no matter where you live, with the missions you'll complete on your own, with a friend or tutor, or as part of the #LanguageHacking community. You can record yourself speaking your scripts aloud in Mandarin and share them with the community where you'll get feedback from other learners and keep the conversation going. This is the best practice you can get – aside from one-to-one conversations with a native speaker. By speaking in front of others you'll become more confident using Mandarin in the real world.

STEP 3: learn from other learners

When you share your missions with other learners, you'll get more comfortable speaking Mandarin – and more importantly, you'll get comfortable speaking the imperfect beginner's Mandarin that everyone must use on the road to fluency. You'll gain insight into how conversations flow in Mandarin, and you'll learn where the 'expression gaps' are in your scripts that you need to fill to expand your conversation skills.

In other words, you'll have everything you need to genuinely start having conversations with other people in Mandarin. After all, isn't that the point?

Let's get started.

WHAT YOU'LL FIND ONLINE

Go to www.teachyourself.co.uk/languagehacking to:

- ···⟫ Download or stream the course audio for free
- ···⟫ Review transcripts for the audio
- ···⟫ Download the literal and approximate translations of the conversations
- ···⟫ Find an up-to-date list of the best free online resources to support your learning
- ···⟫ Link directly to the #LanguageHacking community

THE LANGUAGE HACKER CONTRACT

In this course you will:

···⟶ **get shortcuts** (#languagehacks) to learn a new **yǔyán** (language) fast
···⟶ **learn the words** and **jùzi** (phrases) you need to have real conversations immediately
···⟶ **gain the confidence** to start speaking **Zhōngwén** (Chinese) from day one
···⟶ **have access** to a **shèqū** (community) of like-minded language learners

That's my side of the bargain. It's what I'm giving you.

Now here's your side of the contract. I recommend you read it every day, so it embeds in your memory and becomes part of who you are.

I will speak Mandarin today and every day – if only a little. It will feel awkward and uncomfortable at times. And that's okay.

I will accept that the only way to speak perfectly is to first make mistakes. The only way to overcome my fear is to face it. The only thing preventing me from speaking Mandarin is ... speaking Mandarin.

I will embrace my inner Tarzan. I will say things in Mandarin like 'I Benny. Me writer. I Ireland.' I'll do this because I'm still learning, and because I don't take myself too seriously. I will communicate effectively instead of perfectly. Over time, I will make massive leaps.

I will build 'me-specific' scripts – mini monologues about myself. I will memorize these scripts and rely on them whenever I'm asked questions. I will discover time and time again that I can manage the most common situations I come across in a new language. I will quickly feel my confidence build as I equip myself with the language I need.

I will speak at every opportunity and be an active participant in the Language Hacking community. I will learn from giving and getting feedback.

I will build my skills, day by day, piece by piece.

I will learn smarter. I will be self-sufficient. I will make learning Mandarin part of my daily routine. I will become fluent faster than I ever imagined possible.

I am a language hacker.

Sign here: _____   Date: _____

1 TALKING ABOUT YOU AND ME

Mission

Imagine this – you've made a trip out to the local Chinese market. As you're checking out at the register, you're feeling brave so you say **nǐ hǎo**. The cashier is thrilled to hear you speak his language, and asks you about yourself – in Mandarin!

Your mission is to have your first basic exchange entirely in Mandarin – for 30 seconds. Be prepared to say your name, where you're from and where you live.

This mission will prepare you for the inevitable questions you'll be asked in any first conversation you might have in Mandarin.

Mission prep

- ⋯⋗ Learn basic phrases for introducing yourself: **nǐ hǎo, wǒ shì** …
- ⋯⋗ Learn how to pronounce the Mandarin tones.
- ⋯⋗ Create simple sentences to talk about yourself, with **wǒ shì, wǒ zhù zài** … and ask questions about someone else.
- ⋯⋗ Develop a conversation strategy: letting someone know you don't understand so you can get clarification.
- ⋯⋗ Learn words for countries and nationalities.
- ⋯⋗ Learn challenging pinyin sounds and your first Chinese characters.

BUILDING SCRIPTS

Most first conversations in a new language are predictable. As a beginner, this is great news for you. We're going to start by building your first 'script' to help you prepare for what you'll need to say most, right away. We'll start slow and build as we move on.

If you've studied Mandarin before, some of the words in this unit may be familiar to you. But we'll be doing much more than just learning words in each unit: we're going to start building 'scripts' – conversational templates you can use again and again. Once you learn a script, you can customize it to your needs. This will help you build your language so you can use it from the start.

#LANGUAGEHACK
learn how to use 'to be' and get a head start using basic sentences

CONVERSATION 1

The first words you'll use in every conversation

Let's follow the story of Lucy, a beginner Mandarin learner. Today Lucy is online having her first Mandarin class with her tutor, Teacher Wang. Your first online conversation can always be a little nerve-wracking, so even though Teacher Wang knows Lucy's name, he makes sure to give his new student the chance to introduce herself.

🔊 **01.01** This is a typical introductory conversation – one you'll have yourself many times. Listen to the way the teacher, Lǎoshī, introduces himself using *wǒ shì*.

Wáng Lǎoshī :	Wéi? Wéi? Nǐ zài ma?
Lucy :	**Wéi,** nǐ hǎo. Nǐ shì Wáng Xiānsheng ma?
Wáng Lǎoshī :	Ā … Nǐ hǎo. Wǒ shì Wáng Lǎoshī.
Lucy :	Wáng Lǎoshī, nǐ hǎo! Wǒ shì Lucy! Wǒ hěn gāoxìng rènshi nǐ.
Wáng Lǎoshī :	Wǒ yě hěn gāoxìng rènshi nǐ.

When you see or hear new Mandarin words for the first time, they are going to seem like random noise. But if you train yourself to look and listen a little closer, you'll realize there's a lot you can figure out based on the context of the conversation. The key is to try to notice the language for yourself.

When you're ready, listen again and try to repeat the conversation you've heard, line by line. It's never too early to start speaking and getting a feel for a new language.

FIGURE IT OUT

1 They both start their introductions with a common expression, **nǐ hǎo**. What do you think **nǐ hǎo** means? _____

2 What phrase do both Teacher Wang and Lucy use to give their names?
   _____

3 What phrase do Teacher Wang and Lucy use to say that they're happy to meet one another after they introduce themselves?
   _____

4 Re-read the dialogue. Which word do you think means 'I' and which word means 'you' in the following sentence: **nǐ hǎo. Wǒ shì Wáng Lǎoshī.**

   I _____ you _____

NOTICE

🔊 **01.02** Listen to the audio and study the table. Try to repeat each word.

Essential phrases for Conversation 1

Notice how sentence structure in Mandarin differs from English. The more you actively think about the different ways Chinese uses word order and expressions, the faster you'll learn.

HACK IT: *word chunks*
Learn phrases in 'chunks' rather than understanding each part of every phrase. For example, the entire phrase **Wǒ hěn gāoxìng rènshi nǐ** means 'It's nice to meet you'. Whenever you learn a go-to phrase like this as an entire chunk, practice speaking it on its own to build muscle memory. It will be hard to pronounce the whole phrase at first – but you WILL get it the more you speak it!

Chinese	Meaning	Literal translation
Wéi	Hello	Hello (on the phone only)
Nǐ hǎo	Hello	You good
Nǐ zài ma?	Are you there?	You located [question marker]?
Nǐ shì ...	You are ...	You are ...
Wǒ shì ...	I am ...	I am ...
Xiānsheng	Mr.	Mr.
Nǐ shì ... ma?	Are you ... ?	You are ... [question marker]?
ā	ah	ah
Wǒ yě hěn gāoxìng rènshi nǐ	Nice to meet you, too.	I too (am) very happy to meet you.
yě	also	also

LEARNING STRATEGY:
Understanding 'the gist' when learning a new language, some words or phrases don't have exact translations from one language to the other. Instead, using approximations or doing translation by meaning are more effective strategies for understanding. This is why we look at the closest approximation with the spirit or meaning implied by what is said rather than a word-for-word translation.

PRACTICE

1   Select which word you would use before the following (see the grammar tip on the next page, if you aren't sure):

   a dà (big)   shì / hěn

   b fángzi (house)   shì / hěn

   c dìfang (place)   shì / hěn

   d xiǎo (small)   shì / hěn

   e cháng (long)   shì / hěn

   f yīfu (clothes)   shì / hěn

2 How would you greet someone on the phone (or in a video chat) in Chinese?

_____ _____

3 The phrase **nǐ hǎo** is another common greeting, and another way of saying 'hello'. Take a look at the literal translation column in the Essential Phrases for Conversation 1 to identify the meaning of each word on its own.

a nǐ   _____

b hǎo   _____

4 In Conversation 1, there is a marker that is added to the end of a sentence to make it a 'yes' or 'no' question. What is it? Find it and circle it.

Once you've done that, consider the following statements.

Nǐ shì Wáng Xiānsheng.   **Nǐ shì xuésheng.**

(You are Mr. Wang.)   (You are a student.)

5 Use the question marker to turn these statements into questions:

a Are you Mr. Wang?

_____ _____

b Are you a student?

_____ _____

6 Take a look at the two ways 'you are' is translated in the following phrases. Write them out in Mandarin here.

a Are you there?   _____   _____

b Are you a student? _____   _____

One indicates location in this context while the other does not. Here are a few more examples:

I am here.	Over there.	I am Lucy.	I am in Germany.
Wǒ zài.	Zài nàli.	Wǒ shì Lucy.	Wǒ zài Déguó.
I am a blogger.	I'm at work.		
Wǒ shì bózhǔ.	Wǒ zài gōngzuò.		

GRAMMAR TIP:
to be or not to be?
By now you've likely noticed that two completely different words are used to say 'am'. These are _shì_ and _hěn_. For now, it's best to memorize these as a part of the chunks they appear in **Wǒ hěn gāoxìng rènshi nǐ** and **Wǒ shì ....** But here's a quick hack to help you understand how these two words are used. **Hěn** is used when it is followed by an adjective. For example, in 'I am very happy to meet you,' **gāoxìng** (happy) is an adjective, a word that describes something or the state of something. So if you wanted to say things like 'I am tired', 'I am hungry' or 'I am smart', you'd use **hěn**. **Shì**, on the other hand, is used when the following word is a noun. As a refresher, nouns can be a person, place, thing or idea. These are words like 'teacher', 'mother', or 'engineer'.

CONVERSATION STRATEGY: _filler words_
Need a strategy to buy yourself some time in a conversation? Sometimes just an extra few seconds can give you the time you need to realize you did actually understand what was said or to find the words you need to reply. In Conversation 1, you'll see **ā** used by Teacher Wang. It's very similar to how you might use 'ah' in English. It's a great word to know to give yourself that extra time.

But ... I'm tone deaf!

A lot of people tell me they don't think they could learn Mandarin because they are tone deaf! Generally, this is because they know from experience that they can't sing very well. True tone-deafness (amusia) is less common than many people think, and not quite the same as singing off-key. More importantly, it's also completely different to not being able to handle Mandarin tones! If you can say 'You are?' differently to 'You are!', as well as recognize the difference, then you are perfectly able to handle Mandarin tones!

The '5th tone' of Mandarin

There are some syllables that don't have any accent mark on them. These are pronounced almost like an afterthought, or like an unstressed syllable in a big word. Some refer to this lack of tone as the 'fifth tone'.

7 How would you translate the following? Write them out in Mandarin here.

a Are you ...? / You are ...   _____   _____

b You're located.   _____   _____

8 Now take a look at how the word **wǒ** ('I') is used in Mandarin in the following phrases. Write them out here.

a I am Teacher Wang.   _____   _____

b Nice to meet you.   _____   _____

PRONUNCIATION: TONES

At this point, you may have noticed that there are marks above each of the vocabulary words that you've learned thus far. They are not accent markings like you'd see in the word 'café.' These are called tone markers and they show which of the four tones you use when pronouncing each word.

Mandarin tones will be one of the easiest things you've ever learned! Okay, maybe that's exaggerated, but the basic concept of tones is definitely not as difficult as some people think.

To start, imagine a toddler who is outside with his father. Suddenly, he sees an airplane and points at it, saying 'Da. Da.' The father doesn't initially see what his son is pointing at, so he asks 'Da?' The son is amazed that his father can't see the plane, so he imitates a bit mockingly 'Da?!' and then finally says with conviction and a determined finger pointed 'Da!'

These are all the Mandarin tones, in the order they are usually taught.

The four tones of Mandarin

The first tone, which the toddler uses to point at the airplane at the beginning, stays level: dā.

The second tone rises like a question: dá?

The third tone falls and rises like a mocking question: dǎ?!

And the fourth and final tone is a falling tone, such as you'd use in a strong affirmation, or in a command you'd give to your dog: dà!

Try it – I'm sure you can pronounce them all!

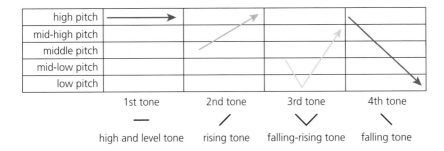

	1st tone	2nd tone	3rd tone	4th tone
	—	╱	╲╱	╲
	high and level tone	rising tone	falling-rising tone	falling tone

Just as in this story, Mandarin tones apply on a per-syllable basis, and that's the real challenge: not to use tones unconsciously anymore as you have been doing in English to add stress or intonation where you want, but to think about them as you speak and choose the right succession of tones for every phrase.

1 🔊 **01.03** Listen to the audio and mimic the four tones. Repeat this exercise several times, then come back and repeat it at least two more times this week.

a mā	má	mǎ	mà	ma	**c** yī	yí	yǐ	yì	yi
b dā	dá	dǎ	dà	da	**d** lē	lé	lě	lè	le

2 🔊 **01.04** Now try recognizing the four different tones. Listen to the audio and write 'level', 'rising', 'falling-rising', or 'falling' for each word. Then listen again and write the corresponding accent marks above each vowel.

a da	_____ _____
b ma	_____ _____
c ni	_____ _____
d zai	_____ _____
e yi	_____ _____
f le	_____ _____

TONES: writing Chinese in letters
To help you figure out which tone is associated with the syllable, pinyin (the system for writing Chinese in Latin letters, which we use in this course) adds little lines above vowels. And these are easy: when the tone stays at the same level, you see a horizontal line, as in **dā**. When the tone rises, the line also rises: **dá**. When the tone falls and rises, the line does the same: **dǎ**. And when the tone falls, the line falls: **dà**.

SPEAKING: *take a risk!*
Language learners often tell me, 'Benny, I've studied for years, but I still can't speak the language!' This happens when you spend all your time reading, listening, or studying ... but not actually speaking Mandarin! Whatever you do, don't study Mandarin in silence. You have to use the language, even if it feels weird or silly, and even if your accent is terrible at first. It will only get better with use! There are lots of ways you can practice using your Mandarin in your community and online. Check out the Resources for some suggestions.

PRACTICE

Making some of these new sounds may feel strange in your mouth, and that's okay – just like riding a bike or driving a car, with regular practice it will become easier and easier.

Scientists have found that saying things out loud makes it more likely for you to remember them, so speaking will boost your memory of Mandarin words and phrases as well.

Don't just study 'in your head' – use every opportunity to actually say the words you're reading out loud!

Say the words below out loud and focus on your pronunciation of the tones.

a wéi

b xiānsheng

c gāoxìng

d xuésheng

e lǎoshī

PUT IT TOGETHER

Let's start building your script. Imagine that you are about to have your very first meeting with a Mandarin tutor online. The language is still fairly new, so you have a limited vocabulary, but in the spirit of Language Hacking you want to get started anyway!

1 Using the conversation as a model, create a short paragraph in which you say to your tutor:

'Hello' (on the phone or online)

Introduce yourself using your name.

Tell them that you are happy to meet them.

Throughout this book, I'll help you keep building this script. You'll draw on this again and again as you start having your first conversations in Mandarin with actual people.

CONVERSATION 2

Tell me ... Where are you from?

When you talk to someone for the first time, you'll need to be prepared to answer basic questions about yourself. As part of their first conversation, Teacher Wang asks Lucy about where she lives and where she's from. Lucy misunderstands what Teacher Wang says about where he lives.

1 ◀))︎ 01.05 Listen to how Lucy uses **ma** here to get more information from Teacher Wang.

> **Wáng Lǎoshī :** Wǒ shì Zhōngguó rén. Lucy, nǐ shì nǎ guó rén?
>
> **Lucy :** Ā ... wǒ shì Jiānádà rén.
>
> **Wáng Lǎoshī :** Wǒ zhù zài Běijīng. Wǒ shì Shànghǎi rén.
>
> **Lucy :** Duìbuqǐ ... Wǒ bù míngbai. Nǐ zhù zài Shànghǎi ma?
>
> **Wáng Lǎoshī :** Wǒ zhù zài Běijīng. Wǒ shì Shànghǎi rén. Nǐ míngbai ma?
>
> **Lucy :** Ā, wǒ míngbai le.
>
> **Wáng Lǎoshī :** Lucy, nǐ zhù nǎli?
>
> **Lucy :** Wǒ zhù zài Zhījiāgē.

CONVERSATION STRATEGY: I'm from ... As a beginner, you need to build towards a basic introductory conversation as your first step. After an initial greeting, a typical first conversation will usually turn towards descriptions about where you're from and where you currently live.

PRONUNCIATION: ZH ZH is pronounced almost the same as the 'j' in the word 'Beijing' or in 'journalist'. If they sound slightly different it's because the tongue is further back for ZH, but as a beginner you can pronounce ZH and j the same.

FIGURE IT OUT

1 How many times do the speakers say 'I am ...'? Find and circle them in the conversation.

You can figure out the answers to all these questions even if you don't know a word of Mandarin, thanks to context and looking at language patterns. Pretty cool, huh?

2 Can you figure out which phrase means 'I live in' ?

_____

_____

3 Where does Lucy live? Circle the word for the correct country and write it out here.

_____

_____

4 What two cities in China does Teacher Wang mention? Which one is he from? Which one does he live in? Circle them and write them out here.

_____

_____

_____

_____

5 Can you work out which phrase means 'I don't understand'? The word 'understand' is used three times in the conversation.

_____

_____

NOTICE

1 🔊 **01.06** Listen to the audio and study the table.

Essential phrases for Conversation 2

Chinese	Meaning	Literal translation
Nǐ shì nǎ guó rén?	Where are you from?	You are what country person?
Nǐ zhù nǎli?	Where do you live?	You live where?
Wǒ shì … rén	I am … person.	I am … person
Wǒ zhù zài …	I live in …	I live located …
Duìbùqǐ	Sorry.	Sorry.
Wǒ (bù) míngbai	I (don't) understand.	I (no) understand
Nǐ míngbai ma?	Do you understand?	You understand [question marker]
le	[change marker]	[change marker] – indicates change of state

2 In Mandarin, how would you say…?

a Canada _____

b Person _____

c Canadian _____

d China _____

e Person _____

f Chinese _____

3 Use the phrase list and write the phrases for ...

   a I am _____ _____

   b I live in _____ _____

   c I understand. _____ _____

   d I'm Canadian. _____ _____

4 Also, notice the language introduced for talking about someone else. Find and write:

   a You live in _____ _____

   b You understand _____ _____

   c You are _____ _____

5 Now look at the placement of the word **bù** for 'not'. Based on that, how do you think you would you say the following?

   a I'm not Chinese. _____ _____

   b I don't understand. _____ _____

   c You don't understand. _____ _____

   d You're not. _____ _____

6 This conversation introduces several phrases you can use to ask someone questions to learn more about them. Find and write the phrases for:

   a Where are you from? _____ _____

   b Where do you live? _____ _____

VOCABULARY:
use rén to say your nationality
Describing your nationality in Mandarin is very simple. You simply say the name of the country you're from followed by the word **rén**, meaning 'person'. Maybe you are German (**Déguó rén** – a Germany person), Australian (**Àodàlìyà rén** – an Australia person), or American (**Měiguó rén** – an America person). This means that just by knowing the name of your country in Mandarin, you can say both the country you live in and, if that's your nationality, where you're from. For example, **Wǒ zhù zài Měiguó. Wǒ shì Měiguó rén.** (I live in America. I'm American!) It can also be used for cities, such as in the example Teacher Wang gave – **Wǒ shì Shànghǎi rén.** (I'm from Shànghǎi.)

One consequence of this simple translation is that the 'dictionary form' that you could look up doesn't actually get the 'to' translated. This will take a little getting used to but if you would ever say 'to' before a verb in English, then you don't have to translate that 'to' in Mandarin: Nǐ huì shuō (You are able to speak, or 'You can speak'). 'To go' is simply 'go' or qù.

#LANGUAGEHACK: learn how to use 'to be' and get a head start using basic sentences

Chinese often gets a bad rap as a difficult language. And while you may encounter aspects of the language different from English that seem difficult, there are also several things about the Chinese language that make it easy.

You may have noticed that the word **shì** appears as a translation of multiple words; **wǒ shì** (I am), **nǐ shì** (you are), **shì shéi** (who is). All of these are forms of 'to be', which is, incidentally, also translated as **shì**.

One of the most wonderful aspects of learning Mandarin, especially compared to learning European languages, is that you never have to learn different forms of verbs (the action/state word of the sentence). This lack of conjugation takes a huge load off that makes learning Mandarin way easier!

Once you know the right single translation of a verb, then that form as you first see it will work without changing, no matter how it is used. Notice how simple this is, once you have the right word:

qù	to go
wǒ qù	I go
nǐ qù	you go
Wáng Lǎoshī qù	Teacher Wang goes
wǒmen qù	we go

VOCABULARY

Here's some new vocabulary to help you to keep building your language script.

1 🔊 **01.07** Listen to the audio and study the table.

BUILDING 'ME-SPECIFIC' LANGUAGE

When you meet a new vocab list (like this one), don't try to memorize all the words – just the ones you can imagine yourself needing in your own conversations. In fact, as you go through this list, go ahead and give yourself the pleasure of striking out with a pencil any words you can't imagine yourself using in the next month or so.

Countries		Cities	
Chinese	**English**	**Chinese**	**English**
Měiguó	America	Niŭyuē	New York
Jiānádà	Canada	Wēngēhuá	Vancouver
Yīngguó	England	Lúndūn	London
Fǎguó	France	Bālí	Paris
Zhōngguó	China	Běijīng	Beijing
Déguó	Germany	Bólín	Berlin
Àodàliyà	Australia	Xīní	Sydney
Yìdàlì	Italy	Luómǎ	Rome
Ài'ěrlán	Ireland	Dūbólín	Dublin
Xībānyá	Spain	Mǎdélǐ	Madrid

If you don't already have one, look online for a good English/Chinese dictionary. The best kinds will allow you to enter English, pinyin, or Chinese characters, and will show you an output of all three. This will help you build vocab that is what I call 'me-specific'. As we go along, you'll need to look up your own words that apply to your life to make your script more useful. Let's start now.

I've listed some good free online dictionaries and apps in the Resources.

1 What countries are you and the people in your life from? Add three new words to each category in the table using words that are specific to you or people close to you.

2 Practice changing countries or cities to nationalities by adding **rén**. Below are a few countries and cities. First, translate them into Mandarin using the table above, then turn them into a nationality.

Germany	Rome	England	Sydney
a _____	b _____	c _____	d _____
from Germany	from Rome	from England	from Sydney
e _____	f _____	g _____	h _____

3 See if you can combine the items we've learned so far in order to say the following things:

a I am French. _____ _____

b I live in France. _____ _____

c Mark is English. _____ _____

d Mark lives in England. _____ _____

e Teacher Wang is Chinese. _____ _____

f I am not American. _____ _____

g I am Irish. _____ _____

h You live in America. _____ _____

i You are not Spanish. _____ _____

Remember, verbs don't change in Mandarin, so 'is' is the same as 'am': shì.

PUT IT TOGETHER

As you're learning new phrases in Mandarin, always think about how you can adapt them for you! Then look up the 'me-specific' words you need to personalize them.

1 Now let's keep building your script. Using the conversation as a model, as well as the vocabulary and 'me-specific' words you have just looked up, create a short paragraph in which you talk about yourself. First, write out in Mandarin:

a what your name is

b where you're from (your nationality)

c where you live.

2 Include a few basic questions for your conversation partner. Write out:

Where are you from?

What is your nationality?

You'll notice we mention both 'Chinese' and 'Mandarin' in this course. Sometimes the terms are interchangeable, but in general 'Chinese' refers to the entire language, especially the written form, while 'Mandarin' refers to just the spoken form of the language.

UNDERSTANDING PINYIN: PART 1

What is pinyin? Pinyin is the system of romanization for the Chinese language. In other words, it is a way of writing in Chinese using Roman or Latin letters. For Chinese learners, pinyin is a helpful system because it gives you the chance to start reading and writing in Chinese without needing to learn characters.

The first pinyin sounds you're going to learn are the more challenging consonants, or initials. That way, after this introduction, everything going forward will get progressively easier. Just because these sounds are more challenging doesn't mean that they're difficult – in fact, many of the sounds also exist in English, so you're already a step ahead. The main difference is that some of the sounds read differently than you're used to as a native English speaker, so it's only a matter of learning to read them with their pinyin pronunciation.

Pinyin is divided into what are known as 'initials' and 'finals'. Initials are usually consonants and finals are either vowels or vowels with a consonant ending. Using shì (to be), the initial would be sh and the final would be i. They combine into one sound, shì. We can also use rén (person) as an example. The initial is r and the final is en. Together they are rén.

1 🔊 **01.08** Here are the sounds. Listen to the audio and study the table.

J	(like jeep)	Sh	(like sure)
Q	(like cheap)	R	(like revision)
X	(like sheep)	Z	(like pizza)
Zh	(like Germany)	C	(like cats)
Ch	(like chirp)	S	(like sip)

2 🔊 **01.09** Listen to the audio and write the initial sound you hear.

a _____   f _____

b _____   g _____

c _____   h _____

d _____   i _____

e _____   j _____

YOUR FIRST CHINESE CHARACTERS

Pinyin is an incredible tool for Chinese learners. You can get really far in your Chinese studies without ever having to learn Chinese characters. And while this course will primarily use pinyin, there's no reason to put off learning characters entirely!

At the end of each unit, I'll teach you some of the most common Chinese characters. Here are a few characters for words you already know.

人 rén

In Chinese, 人 (**rén**) can mean: 'man', 'person', or 'people'. You saw it in the section on nationalities – adding 人 (**rén**) to a country makes it a nationality. That's because you are literally saying '[place] person', or 'person from this place'.

The character 人 (**rén**) resembles the side view of a person walking. It has two strokes. They are written in this order:

人
rén
(2 strokes)

¹ 丿	² 人			

Generally, strokes go from top to bottom, left to right and horizontal to vertical.

Practice writing this character in the space below.

不 bù

To say 'no, not' or to make something negative, you add 不 (bù) in Chinese. You saw this word in **wǒ bù míngbai** – (I don't understand). Imagine the line on the top as the top of a birdcage – the bird inside can not fly higher than the top of the cage. This character has four strokes and they are written as follows:

bù (bú)
(4 strokes)

Practice writing this character in the space below.

中 zhōng

The Chinese character 中 (zhōng) can mean: 'within', 'among', 'in', 'middle', 'center,' 'while (doing something)', or 'during'. Imagine dividing a rectangle into two equal halves, down the middle. You learned it as a part of **Zhōngguó**, the Chinese word for 'China' because the Chinese word for 'China' is actually 'Middle Kingdom'. **Zhōng** means 'middle' and **guó** means 'kingdom'. This character has four strokes that are written in the following order:

 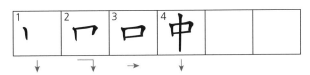

zhōng
(4 strokes)

Practice writing this character in the space below.

COMPLETING UNIT 1

Check your understanding

🔊 01.10 Go back and re-read the conversations. Then, when you're feeling confident, listen to the audio rehearsal below, which will ask you questions and prompt you to have a conversation in Mandarin.

LEARNING STRATEGY:
active listening
When you do a listening exercise, make sure you actively pay attention to the audio. A common mistake is to listen to Mandarin audio 'in the background', thinking it will still 'sink in'. The truth is, there's a huge difference between hearing a language and listening to a language. Make sure 100% of your attention is on the audio while it plays!

⋯⊹ pause or replay the audio as often as you need to understand the questions

⋯⊹ repeat after the speaker until the pronunciation feels and sounds natural to you

⋯⊹ answer the questions in Mandarin (in complete sentences)

Teacher: Hello! I'm Teacher Sarah.

Student: Hello! I'm _____ _____.

Teacher: Nice to meet you.

Student: Nice to meet you, too!

Teacher: Are you Canadian?

Student: I'm Canadian. / No, I'm … Where are you from?

Teacher: I'm Chinese. Do you understand?

Student: [Say you understand!]

Teacher: Where do you live?

Student: I live in [country]. Where do you live?

Teacher: I live in China.

Each unit will build on the previous one, helping you to review as you move ahead. Pause or replay the audio as often as you need to understand the questions. Do your best to answer in complete sentences.

Show what you know...

Here's what you've just learned. Write or say an example for each item in the list. Then check off the ones you know.

- ☑ Say hello!   Nǐ hǎo.
- ☐ Introduce yourself.
- ☐ Say which country you're from.
- ☐ Say where you live.

COMPLETE YOUR MISSION

It's time to complete your mission: giving a basic introduction to yourself entirely in Mandarin – for 30 seconds. To do this, you'll need to prepare your answers to the questions you'll most likely be asked.

STEP 1: build your script

Start your script with the phrases you learned in this unit, combined with 'me-specific' vocabulary, to answer common questions about yourself. Be sure to:

···⟫ Say your name using **wǒ shì**.
···⟫ Say where you're from and where you live, using **wǒ shì … rén** and **wǒ zhù zài**.

Write down your script, then repeat it until you feel confident.

STEP 2: real language hackers speak from day one … online

If you're feeling good about your script, it's time to complete your mission and share a recording of you speaking your script with the community. So, go online, find the mission for Unit 1 and give it your best shot.

STEP 3: learn from other learners

How well can you understand someone else's introduction? After you've uploaded your own clip, check out what the other people in the community have to say about themselves. Your task is to ask a follow-up question in Mandarin to at least three different people.

STEP 4: reflect on what you learned

What did you find easy or difficult about this unit? Did you learn any new words or phrases in the community space? After every script you write or conversation you have, you'll gain a lot of insight on what 'gaps' you need to fill in your script. Always write them down!

HEY, LANGUAGE HACKER, LOOK AT YOU GO!

You've only just started on the new path to language hacking, and you've already learned so much. You've taken the first crucial steps, and started to interact with others using Mandarin. This is something other students don't do even after years of studying, so you should be truly proud of yourself.

In just one unit of this book, you've already started to discover other methods for learning Mandarin that work for you and bring you closer to your goal. Being unintimidated by the learning process is one of the most crucial parts of getting into language learning. Now that you see how straightforward learning Mandarin can be, let's forge ahead!

Jiāyóu is a Mandarin expression for cheering someone on. It's similar to 'keep it up!' in English, but literally means 'add oil'.

→ Jiāyóu!

2 ASKING ABOUT YOU

Mission

Imagine this – your friend brings you to the park to try a lesson in the Chinese martial art **tàijí quán** in Mandarin. You want to blend in and not rely on English.

Your mission is to trick someone into thinking you're a confident Mandarin speaker for at least 30 seconds. Be prepared to strike up a conversation and talk about the languages you speak or those you want to learn. After the 30 seconds have passed, you reveal how long you've been learning Mandarin and dazzle them! To avoid arousing suspicion, keep the other person talking by asking casual questions to show your interest.

This mission will give you the confidence to initiate conversations with new people.

Mission prep

- Ask and respond to questions using: **shì bu shì**.
- Turn the conversation around with: **nǐ ne**?
- Use the question words: **shénme, qǐngwèn, duōjiǔ le**?
- Develop a conversation strategy using filler words (**nà**) to create conversational flow.
- Learn 11 more pinyin sounds, time periods and the numbers 1-10.
- Learn four Chinese characters for numbers.

BUILDING LANGUAGE FOR ASKING QUESTIONS

Let's learn the simple (but effective!) technique of bouncing back a question with **nǐ ne** and learn to ask more specific questions using several new question words.

#LANGUAGEHACK
learn vocab faster with memory hooks

No matter where you live in the world, there are other Mandarin learners nearby who want to practice Mandarin with you. You can also find native speakers to help you learn. See our Resources to learn how to connect with other Mandarin learners and speakers.

As a beginner, you need to build towards an introductory conversation as your first step. After an initial greeting, a conversation will usually turn to where you're from and where you live, and what languages you speak.

Remember: you can attach **rén** to locations – whether cities, states or countries – to let someone know where you're from!

CONVERSATION STRATEGY:

umm....

Need extra time figuring out what to say or find the right words? You can use filler words to buy yourself some time. Lucy uses **nà** which is similar to the way you might use 'so ...' at the beginning of a sentence in English.

CONVERSATION 1

Words you'll need to ask questions

A week into her stay in China, Lucy attends a language learners' meet-up near her house. There, she meets Xiǎowēi, a Beijinger. After the initial introductions, Lucy and her new friend start to talk about their language skills. Xiǎowēi mentions **Hányǔ** (Korean) and **Guǎngdōnghuà** (Cantonese). Pay attention to their endings.

🔊 **02.01** Note the way Xiǎowēi and Lucy ask one another questions.

To remember that this word means 'English', you can hear that the first part actually sounds a little like the first syllable of English. When I first heard the second part, it sounded a little like an impressed 'oooh!' that I imagined the Alien toys say in reaction to seeing Buzz Lightyear in the first Toy Story film. This 'alien communication' association helped me to remember that it meant 'language.' You can also see **yǔ** used in **Fǎyǔ** (French) and **Hányǔ** (Korean).

Xiǎowēi : Qǐngwèn, nǐ shì **Zhījiāgē rén**, shì bu shì?

Lucy : Wǒ bú shì Zhījiāgē rén. Wǒ shì Duōlúnduō rén.

Xiǎowēi : A, wǒ míngbai le. Nà, nǐ huì shuō Fǎyǔ, shì bu shì?

Lucy : Bú huì shuō. Wǒ zhǐ huì shuō **Yīngyǔ**, yìdiǎn Zhōngwén. Nǐ ne?

Xiǎowēi : Wǒ huì shuō Hányǔ. Guǎngdōnghuà yě bu **cuò**.

Lucy : Nà nǐ bú huì shuō Yīngyǔ ma?

Xiǎowēi : Hái bú huì. Jīntiān wǒ yào liànxí yíxià.

VOCABULARY: cuò

The Chinese word **cuò** has several ways it can be translated back into English. 'Bad', 'mistake' and 'false' are three of the most common ways you'll see it used. For example: **Zhè shì wǒ de cuò** means 'that's my fault'. **Wǒ cuò le** means 'I made a mistake' and **duì huòzhě cuò** means 'true or false'.

FIGURE IT OUT

1 Use the context to figure out:

    a How many languages does Xiǎowēi speak?   two / three

    b Is Lucy from Montreal?   **shì** (yes) / **bú shì** (no)

    c How many languages does Lucy speak?   two / three

2 Are these statements about the conversation true (**duì**) or false (**cuò**)?

    a Lucy does not speak French (**Fǎyǔ**).   **duì / cuò**

    b Xiǎowēi speaks Cantonese (**Guǎngdōnghuà**).   **duì / cuò**

    c Lucy is from Toronto.   **duì / cuò**

    d Xiǎowēi wants to practice English (**Yīngyǔ**).   **duì / cuò**

3 What phrase does Xiǎowēi use in the third line to confirm she understood Lucy?

_____

_____

4 What expression does Lucy use to ask Xiǎowēi 'and you?'.

_____

_____

5 What 'pause' or 'filler' word does Xiǎowēi use when asking Lucy if she speaks French?

_____

_____

GRAMMAR STRATEGY: SAYING YES/NO

In Chinese, there's no direct translation for 'yes' and 'no'. Instead, you make the verbs work for you. This means that when someone asks you a question, you can simply use the verb to affirm or negate the question asked with *bù*.

For example, **Nǐ huì shuō Yīngyǔ ma**? (Can you speak English? lit. 'you able speak English [question marker]?')

Yes   **Huì**

No   **Bú huì**

Nǐ shì Zhōngguó rén ma? (Are you Chinese?)

Yes   Shì

No   Bú shì

Try it! Answer the following questions by repeating the verb used in the question in its affirmative or negative form.

1 Nǐ shì Měiguó rén ma? (Are you American?)

2 Nǐ huì shuō Fǎyǔ ma? (Can you speak French?)

3 Nǐ míngbai ma? (Do you understand?)

NOTICE

🔊 02.02 Listen to the audio and study the table.

Essential phrases for Conversation 1

Chinese	Meaning	Literal translation
qǐngwèn	may I ask	please ask
shì bu shì?	is that right?	is not is?
Nà ...	then ...	then ...
huì shuō	can speak	able to speak ('able' implies they have a skill)
zhǐ	only	only
yìdiǎn	a little	a little (often connected to nouns)
yíxià	a bit	a bit (often connected to verbs)
yě	also	also
Nǐ ne?	And you?	You [marker]?
bú cuò	not bad	no mistake
hái bú huì	not yet	still not able
jīntiān	today	today
wǒ yào liànxí	I want to practice	I want practice

GRAMMAR TIP:
a little

In Chinese there are a few different ways to say 'a little' or 'a bit', and which one you'll use will depend on the context. **Yìdiǎn** is often used in connection with nouns or adjectives. In other words, you would say **Yìdiǎn Zhōngwén** (a little Chinese) but **màn Yìdiǎn** (a little slower). Whereas **yíxià** is used to say that the duration of something was or will be short as in **liànxí yíxià** (to practice a little) or **shuō yíxià** (to speak for a little).

LEARNING STRATEGY:
remember to use short sentences!

Whenever you want to express multiple things – like the fact you speak English and a little French – remember to use shorter sentences. This simplifies what grammar you'll need to use and helps your conversations go more smoothly. This may be different from what you're used to, but don't worry about it! If you forget and find yourself lost mid-sentence, people can usually still understand you. As you read through this book, you'll notice the word-for-word translations, and you'll start to get a feel for how the language works.

1 Re-read the conversation, then write out in Mandarin the sentence Lucy
  uses to say she 'only' speaks English and a little Chinese:

  _____

  _____

2 Choose whether you would use **yìdiǎn** or **yíxià** in the following
  examples by circling the correct choice:

  a a little French   **yìdiǎn / yíxià**

  b to practice for a bit   **yìdiǎn / yíxià**

  c to ask for a bit   **yìdiǎn / yíxià**

3 Circle and write the Chinese phrases meaning:

  a not yet   _____ _____

  b not bad   _____ _____

  c also   _____ _____

  d may I ask   _____ _____

4 What word means 'can' in the sense that someone has the ability to
  learn something?

  _____

5 Use what you remember about **bù** to negate a sentence and complete
  the sequence in Chinese:

  a ___ ___ am   ⟶   **b** ___ ___ am not

  c ___ ___ understand ⟶   **d** ___ ___ don't understand

  e ___ ___ can speak   ⟶   **f** ___ ___ can't speak

  g ___ ___ want   ⟶   **h** ___ ___ don't want

GRAMMAR EXPLANATION: ASKING QUESTIONS

So far, you've learned three ways to ask questions in Chinese. The first
way is by adding **ma** to the end of a sentence to turn it into a question.
This is only used for 'yes' or 'no' questions.

The second way to form a question is to add **shì bu shì** (isn't it?) to the
end of the sentence. Using this structure is a way to confirm information.
If, for example, you're not sure how to say 'how is the weather?' you can
instead say 'the weather is nice today, isn't it?' to get the information
you're looking for.

We do this in English too with certain questions. 'This is delicious, isn't it?', 'You're tired, aren't you?'

The third way you learned to ask a question in the dialogue was by using **Nǐ ne?** (And you?). After sharing something about yourself or someone else, you can add this to find out the same information about the person you're talking to. For example: 'I'm Irish. And you?'

1 Turn the following into questions by adding **ma**:

a _____ _____ you understand ⟶ b _____ _____ Do you understand?

c _____ _____ I want ⟶ d _____ _____ Do I want?

e _____ _____ Lucy can speak ⟶ f _____ _____ Can Lucy speak
Chinese. Chinese?

2 Turn the following into questions by adding **shì bu shì**:

a _____ _____ You are ⟶ b _____ _____ You are American,
American. aren't you?

c _____ _____ You live in ⟶ d _____ _____ You live in Beijing,
Beijing. don't you?

e _____ _____ Lucy practices ⟶ f _____ _____ Lucy practices a bit,
a bit. doesn't she?

3 Turn the statement around by adding 'and you'?

a I am French. And you? _____ _____

b I live in Germany. And you? _____ _____

c I am George. And you? _____ _____

PRACTICE

1 Practice using the vocab you've learned! Fill in the missing word(s) in Chinese.

a Nǐ _____ Méngtèlì'ěr rén. (You are from Montreal.)

b Nǐ _____ shuō Fǎyǔ. (You are able to speak French.)

c Hái _____ huì. (Still / not yet able.)

d Wǒ yào liànxí _____ (I want to practice a bit.)

e Lucy míngbai le, _____? (Lucy understands, doesn't she?)

2 🔊 **02.03** Practice recognizing the difference in structure between questions and statements in Mandarin. You'll hear the three sentence structures you've learned so far:

Questions using **ma**

Questions using the **shì bu shì** structure

Statements that are turned around with: **Nǐ ne?**

Listen to the audio and select W if you hear a **wèntí** (question), and D if you hear a **dá'àn** (answer) or general statement.

a W / D   **b** W / D   **c** W / D

d W / D   **e** W / D   **f** W / D

PUT IT TOGETHER

1 You should always be learning new Mandarin vocab of your own! Use a dictionary to look up the Mandarin translations for the languages given. Then add two more languages in Chinese that you would like to learn.

a Japanese _____   **b** German _____   **c** French _____

d Russian _____   **e** _____   **f** _____

2 If you speak other languages, say whether you speak them 'not bad' or only 'a little bit'. If you want to learn other languages, say which ones. Write out your answers here in Chinese. Then repeat them out loud.

a Qǐngwèn, nǐ huì shuō Yīngyǔ ma?

Huì / bú huì, _____ _____

b Nǐ huì shuō Zhōngwén, shì bu shì?

(Say you speak a little.) _____ _____

c Nǐ huì shuō Fǎyǔ ma?

_____ _____

#LANGUAGEHACK: learn vocab faster with memory hooks

You may think you don't have the memory to learn lots of new words. But you absolutely can! The trick I use for remembering new vocab is mnemonics, or memory hooks.

A mnemonic is a learning tool that helps you remember a lot more words and phrases. You can see an example I gave for how to remember **yǔ** (language) already.

While **yǔ** is used for most foreign languages, you'll have noticed that one way to say 'Chinese/Mandarin' is **Zhōngwén**. If you've had trouble recalling this word, then try the following technique:

I imagined old-time cowboy actor John Wayne, because his name sounds a little similar to **Zhōngwén**. If you can't picture him, then imagine any other John you can think of, who is maybe looking out of a window.

As you can see, I come up with words in English that sound a little similar, so I can get the pronunciation close. From there, I try to visualize some kind of story that helps me burn the tones into my mind and tie it in with the actual meaning so it jumps out at me when recalling the mnemonic.

For instance, I imagine John Wayne (or another John) looking out a window, seeing a charging member of the Terracotta Army (famous stone soldiers found near Xian, in the middle of China, and representing the language in this association). John shoots his gun at him, but the soldier reacts quickly with his swords and knocks the bullet so hard it flies off diagonally towards the sky.

As I think back on this, then the path the bullet takes will help me remember the tones of the two components of **Zhōngwén**. First, it flies out directly horizontal, and then it goes upwards.

An odd story, right? But with the mnemonic technique, the stranger it is, the better it works. And while long to explain here, it takes but a few seconds to conjure it all up in my mind and say the word!

These associations act like glue for your memory. The key to a good mnemonic is to think about an image or sound that connects the word to its meaning. Then try to make it silly, dramatic or shocking – make it memorable! Simply say the Chinese word out loud until you can think of an English word that sounds like it. (It may even be similar in meaning.) Then you can attach a powerful (silly, weird or funny) image to it – anything that helps.

Examples:

To remember that **jīntiān** means 'today', I imagined myself writing on a calendar to wear 'jeans' to drink 'tea' with a friend today.

To remember that **liànxí** means 'practice', I simply thought of a lioness (lion-'she') banging its paws down and up on a piano (down and up to mimic the tones), to practice playing it.

YOUR TURN: Use the hack

🔊 02.04 Listen to the audio to hear the pronunciation of each word. Repeat the words and then use sound or image association to create your own mnemonics. They don't have to be logical, or even make sense to other people, as long as they're memorable to you.

I'll occasionally hint at tricks you can use to remember new vocab. For now, you should get used to creating new mnemonics yourself!

a **jiē** (street)

b **yuèliang** (moon)

c **guì** (expensive)

d **dōngxi** (thing)

e **hǎoxiào** (funny)

CONVERSATION 2

How long have you been learning Mandarin?

Another 'first question' you can expect when you speak Mandarin with someone new is 'How long have you been learning Chinese?' In the next conversation, Lucy is speaking with Xiǎowēi about her Chinese studies and what languages she would like to learn next.

🔊 02.05 Let's prepare your response to that question now. Can you identify how Xiǎowēi asks Lucy, 'How long ...' in her second line?

When looking at a new conversation, first try to identify all the words you know. That will make figuring out the other words in the sentence much easier!

To remember that this means 'like' (here, 'you like'), I thought of one of life's greatest pleasures – for me personally – fresh sheets on my bed. Then I imagine a magic 'sheet wand' that helps me make the bed. To remember the tones, I imagine flapping it out over the bed making a shape similar to the tone on **xǐ**. I then picture myself holding a magic wand straight out horizontally so the sheet falls perfectly into place. I then dive into the bed saying 'I like this!' as I get comfy thanks to my 'sheet-wand'.

> **Xiǎowēi :** Qǐngwèn, Lucy, nǐ xǐhuan zhù zài Běijīng ma?
>
> **Lucy :** Xǐhuan.
>
> **Xiǎowēi :** Nǐ xué Zhōngwén duōjiǔ **le**?
>
> **Lucy :** Wǒ yǐjing xué le shí tiān le.
>
> **Xiǎowēi :** Zhǐ yǒu shí tiān? Tài bàng le!
>
> **Lucy :** Hái xíng ba. Wǒ xǐhuan xué **yǔyán**.
>
> **Xiǎowēi :** Nǐ yào xué shénme yǔyán?
>
> **Lucy :** Wǒ yào xué Zhōngwén, Rìyǔ hé Éyǔ.
>
> **Xiǎowēi :** Éyǔ hěn nán, shì bu shì?
>
> **Lucy :** Wǒ xǐhuan tiǎozhàn.

GRAMMAR TIP:

plurals

When it comes to handling plurals, Chinese does things much more simply than English. For example, 'language' is **yǔyán** and 'languages' is also **yǔyán**. This means that you don't have to worry about what spelling changes need to happen for plurals or what rules to follow – the word stays the same!

GRAMMAR TIP:

... how long?

In English, 'how long ...' comes at the beginning of the sentence. In Chinese, it comes at the end. An easy way to remember this is by rephrasing how you'd say this in English. For example, 'You study Chinese! How long?' Or 'You live in Beijing! How long?' This hack will help you turn any statement into a 'how long' question.

FIGURE IT OUT

1 Use the context along with what you've learned in Unit 1 to figure out:

a Does Lucy enjoy living in Beijing? Circle her answer in the conversation, then write it out here:

_____

_____

b In the dialogue, there are the names of several languages. Find and circle them.

2 Write out the Chinese expressions in Conversation 2. Look for clues, like where each phrase would be in the sentence, punctuation marks, words you already know, and logical conclusion to a conversation.

a 'may I ask' (first line) _____ _____

b 'that's amazing!' _____ _____

c 'challenge' _____ _____

3 Use the context to figure out if Xiǎowēi thinks Russian is a hard language. Does she think it's difficult?

Yes / No

NOTICE

🔊 **02.06** Listen to the audio and study the table.

Essential phrases for Conversation 2

Chinese	Meaning	Literal translation
xǐhuan	like	like
xué le	studied	study [marker]
... duōjiǔ le?	how long ...?	... how long [marker]?
yǐjing	already	already
shí tiān	ten days	ten day
zhǐ yǒu	it's only been / there's only	only has
Tài bàng le!	That's amazing!	too amazing [marker]
Hái xíng ba.	I'm okay, I guess.	still okay [suggestion marker]
yǔyán	language(s)	language
shénme	what	what
hěn nán	is hard	very hard
tiǎozhàn	challenge	challenge

> **VOCABULARY:**
> *tài bàng le*
> **Tài bàng le** is an extremely versatile phrase. Whenever you think something is cool or impressive, you can use it.

'But my Chinese is bad!'
Chinese speakers are often excited you are learning their language, so they'll shower you with compliments on your language skills (even if you've only spoken a word or two). Here, Xiǎowēi compliments Lucy on how quickly she's learned Mandarin, and Lucy shows how she handles a compliment humbly. In Chinese culture, it's common to deflect compliments rather than accept them with thanks. Another phrase you could use is **hái hǎo ba** (it's alright, I guess).

> **HACK IT: *double your vocab with bù***
> Since you know the word **bù**, you've practically doubled your vocab with a shortcut for saying opposites. Imagine you want to tell your Chinese friend, 'this is easy', but you haven't learned the word 'easy' yet. You can simply say it's 'not hard'. **Bù nán.**

1 When starting a conversation with Xiǎowēi, Lucy uses a word to politely get her attention. Circle the word and write it here.

_____

2 You learned a couple of new action words in this conversation. Write them in Chinese below.

   a to study _____

   b to like _____

3 How many languages does Lucy want to learn? (Find the words with **yǔ**.)

_____

What are they? Write the Chinese words for the languages in the space below. Can you guess what they are in English?

_____

_____

_____

4 Xiǎowēi and Lucy use several expressions to share their thoughts and interest. Find them in the conversation and write them in Chinese below.

a It's okay _____ _____

b It's not bad _____ _____

c … is hard _____ _____

PRACTICE 1

1 🔊 **02.07** Read the following words out loud to practice your pronunciation. Then listen to the native pronunciation to see if you got it right.

a zhù, Zhōngwén, zhǐ

b duōjiǔ, jiē, yǐjing

c xué, cuò, xǐhuan

2 Find the phrase 'how long?' in the list. Circle it, then write it here.

_____

_____

3 How do you say the following in Chinese? Listen and find them in the conversation. Then write the expressions in Chinese.

a already _____   **b** It's only been _____   **c** okay _____

4 🔊 **02.08** Listen to the audio and study the Numbers and Time periods tables.

Numbers (0-10)

Mandarin	yī	èr	sān	sì	wǔ	liù	qī	bā	jiǔ	shí	líng
Meaning	one	two	three	four	five	six	seven	eight	nine	ten	zero

Time periods

Chinese	Meaning
sì tiān	four days
sì ge xīngqī	four weeks
sì ge yuè	four months
sì nián	four years

GRAMMAR TIP: *measure words*

Chinese uses measure words, but before you worry about this new grammar point, know that English uses measure words, too! We have 'a loaf of bread', 'a bag of chips', 'a ream of paper', 'a herd of horses', 'a school of fish', 'a pod of dolphins', 'a gaggle of geese' and 'a murder of crows'. In Chinese, the most common measure word is **ge** – it's used for people, time and for almost any noun when you can't think of an alternative.

5 Translate the following into Chinese:

a **Example.** Nine days <u>jiǔ tiān</u>

b Three weeks _____ _____

c Six months _____ _____

d Eight months _____ _____

e Ten years _____ _____

f Five days _____ _____

PRACTICE 2

1 Translate the following sentences into Chinese. Use the tables to help you.

How long have you studied French?

Example. <u>Nǐ xué Fǎyǔ duōjiǔ le?</u>

a I have been studying Chinese for three months.

_____

_____

b How long have you been living in Beijing?

_____

_____

c I am learning Russian and French.

_____

_____

2 Can you think of some interesting mnemonics for the following words? (Focus on the pronunciation, rather than the spelling.)

sān	líng	qī
three	zero	seven

PRACTICE 3

Let's use what you've learned to prepare a cheat sheet with the numbers and times of the year you're likely to use when talking about yourself. Keep coming back to the cheat sheet to add information as you go along.

	Useful phrases	My info
Age	Wǒ ... suì (I'm ... years old)	
How long I've been learning Chinese		
Month you started learning Chinese		

1 Look up the number that corresponds to your age and add it to the cheat sheet. How old are you in Chinese?

2 Months in Chinese are easy! You simply take the number of the month and add **yuè**. For example, February is **èr yuè** and July is **qī yuè**. What month did you start learning Chinese? Add it to the table.

Example.

Zài èr yuè (in February) _____ _____

3 Look up other important numbers in your life and add them to your cheat sheet! For instance, you might add:

how many children/cats you have

how many languages you speak.

4 Now create an entire sentence that's true for you. Respond to the question by saying how many days, weeks, months or years you've been learning Chinese.

Nǐ xué Zhōngwén duōjiǔ le?

_____

_____

HACK IT: *learn vocab strategically*
Remember, you don't need to memorize all of the numbers or other types of vocab in Chinese right away. Start by thinking about what you'll need to say most often, and learn that first. The rest will come with time, and conversation!

BUILDING 'ME-SPECIFIC' LANGUAGE

Languages, like nationalities, are formed from the word for the country. You simply replace **guó** (country) with **yǔ**, **wén**, or **huà** (all mean 'language') depending on the language. For example, **Yīngguó** (England) becomes **Yīngyǔ** (English). Here's some new vocabulary to help you to keep building your language script.

Preview the table below and fill in the missing languages. At the end of the table, add three of your own countries and languages.

Countries		Languages	
Yīngguó	England	Yīngyǔ	English
Guǎngzhōu*	Canton	Guǎngdōnghuà	Cantonese
Rìběn	Japan	Rìyǔ	Japanese
Hánguó	Korea	_____	Korean
Éguó	Russia	_____	Russian
Zhōngguó	China	_____	Chinese
Déguó	Germany	_____	German
Fǎguó	France	_____	French
_____	_____	_____	_____
_____	_____	_____	_____
_____	_____	_____	_____

* The capital of a large province in China with its own language.

PUT IT TOGETHER

Use what you've just learned, along with any new 'me-specific' vocab you've looked up, to write four sentences about yourself.

Write how long you've been learning Chinese using **xué**.

⋯⇥ Use **Wǒ huì shuō** to share which languages you can speak.

⋯⇥ Use **Wǒ ... suì** to say how old you are.

UNDERSTANDING PINYIN: PART 2

Previously, you learned the more challenging consonants and now you'll learn the easy sounds. Why are they easy? Because they sound very much like English letters you already know.

1 🔊 **02.09** Here are the sounds. Listen to the audio and study the table.

B (like bump)	**N** (like nut)
P (like pump)	**L** (like love)
M (like mother)	**G** (like gumption)
F (like fun)	**K** (like kangaroo)
D (like dub)	**H** (like hunger)
T (like touch)	

2 🔊 **02.10** Listen to the audio and write the initial sounds you hear.

a _____   g _____

b _____   h _____

c _____   i _____

d _____   j _____

e _____   k _____

f _____

MORE CHINESE CHARACTERS

In this unit, you learned your first Chinese numbers so it's the perfect time to learn your first characters for numbers. Let's dive in!

一 yī

The character for 'one' in Chinese is 一. It's easy to remember because it's one horizontal stroke.

This character only has one stroke. It's drawn from left to right:

yī (yí; yì)
(1 stroke)

Practice writing this character in the space below.

二 èr

The Chinese character for 'two' is as easy to remember as 'one'. It's two horizontal strokes. The top stroke is slightly shorter than the bottom stroke and it's drawn first.

'Two' has two strokes. They are written in this order:

èr
(2 strokes)

Practice writing this character in the space below.

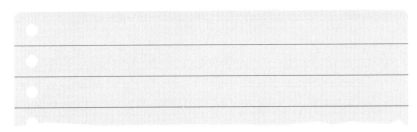

三 sān

If you guessed that 'three' would be a character made up of three horizontal strokes, you guessed correctly. Here's where the pattern ends. The remaining numbers do not continue to follow this pattern. With 'three', the third and bottom stroke is, like with 'two', the longest.

The number three is written with three strokes. They are written in this order:

三 sān
(3 strokes)

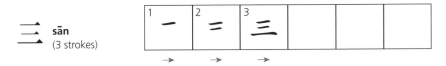

Practice writing this character in the space below.

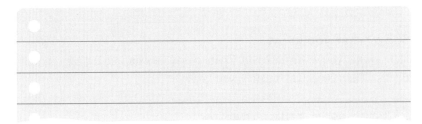

十 shí

The last character you'll learn today is the character for 'ten' in Chinese. It looks very similar to a plus sign. Can you think of any fun mnemonics to remember how to draw this character?

The character for 'ten' is written in two strokes. They are drawn in this order:

十 shí
(2 strokes)

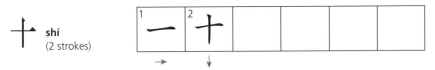

Practice writing this character in the space below.

COMPLETING UNIT 2

Check your understanding

🔊 02.11 Go back and reread the conversations. When you're feeling confident:

⋯⁖ listen to the audio rehearsal, which will ask you questions and prompt you to have a conversation in Mandarin.

⋯⁖ pause or replay the audio as often as you need to understand the questions.

⋯⁖ repeat after the speaker until the pronunciation feels and sounds natural to you.

⋯⁖ answer the questions in Mandarin (in complete sentences).

Remember you can always use filler words like nà or ā to give yourself time to think!

Show what you know...

Here's what you've just learned. Write or say an example for each item in the list. Then check off the ones you know.

☐ How to politely preface a question.
☐ How to confirm if a statement is correct or not.
☐ How to say if you can speak a language.
☐ Ask the question 'how long have you been learning Chinese?'
☐ Say how long you've been learning Chinese.
☐ Numbers from 0 to 10.
☐ Say what other languages you speak or want to learn.
☐ Negate a sentence using bù.
☐ Pronounce 11 new pinyin initials.
☐ Use mnemonics to remember tricky vocab.
☐ The Chinese characters for numbers 1, 2, 3 and 10.

COMPLETE YOUR MISSION

It's time to complete your mission: trick someone into thinking you speak Mandarin for at least 30 seconds, by striking up conversation about the languages you speak and what languages you want to learn. To do this, you'll need to prepare to initiate a conversation by asking questions and replying with your own answers.

STEP 1: build your script

Keep building your script by writing out some 'me-specific' sentences along with some common questions you might ask someone else. Be sure to:

···⁚ ask a question using **duōjiǔ le**? or **shì bu shì**?
···⁚ ask a question using **qǐngwèn** at the start
···⁚ say how long you've been learning Chinese using **xué**
···⁚ say whether or not you speak other languages and how well you speak them
···⁚ say what other languages you want to learn
···⁚ write down your script, then repeat it until you feel confident.

STEP 2: all the cool kids are doing it ... online.

You've put the time into preparing your script, now it's time to complete your mission and share your recording with the community. Go online to find the mission for Unit 2 and use the Chinese you've learned right now!

STEP 3: learn from other learners.

How well can you understand someone else's script? Your task is to listen to at least two clips uploaded by other learners. How long have they been learning Chinese? Do they speak any other languages? Leave a comment in Chinese saying which words you were able to understand and answering a question they ask at the end of their video. And ask them one of the questions you've prepared.

STEP 4: reflect on what you learned.

What did you find easy or difficult in this unit?

After only two missions, you've learned so many words and phrases you can use in real conversations. Don't forget that you can mix and match words and sentences to create endless combinations. Get creative!

HEY, LANGUAGE HACKER, DO YOU REALIZE HOW MUCH YOU CAN ALREADY SAY?

In the next few units, you'll learn more about how to have conversations in Mandarin – even if you have a limited vocab or haven't been learning for very long.

3 I LIKE SPEAKING MANDARIN

Mission

Imagine this – you had a great time at **tàijí quán** and you were invited by a new friend to go to a party that evening. At the party, someone decides to play a party game – describe something without saying the word itself!

Your mission is to use your limited language and win the game. Be prepared to use 'Tarzan Mandarin' and other conversation strategies to describe a celebrity based on what they do (play soccer, sing or act) and where they're from.

This mission will help you overcome the fear of imperfection and show you how with just a few words and a powerful technique, you can make yourself understood.

Mission prep

- ⋯⋗ Use new phrases for introducing yourself: **Wǒ jiào ...**
- ⋯⋗ Use survival phrases to ask for help with your Chinese: **Wǒ tīng bú dào**
- ⋯⋗ Discuss your hobbies: **Nǐ yǒu shénme àihào?**
- ⋯⋗ Talk about what you like or don't like: **Wǒ xǐhuan / Wǒ bù xǐhuan.**
- ⋯⋗ Use question words to learn more about the people you meet.
- ⋯⋗ Learn pinyin finals.
- ⋯⋗ Learn four new Chinese characters.

BUILDING LANGUAGE FOR MEETING SOMEONE NEW

Practicing your Mandarin with a tutor or exchange partner online, especially when you don't live in a Mandarin-speaking country, is one of the most effective (and affordable) ways to learn more Mandarin in a shorter amount of time. You can do this right away, even if you don't know many phrases yet. In this unit you'll learn strategic survival phrases you can use whenever there's something you don't understand, and you'll use 'Tarzan Mandarin' to communicate with limited language or grammar. Strategies like these help you become comfortable making mistakes when speaking, and help you have meaningful conversations despite being a beginner.

#LANGUAGEHACK
get a head start with words you already know

CONVERSATION 1

Having an online chat

Lucy has decided to get some extra Mandarin practice and she's about to have her next online conversation with Jùnfēng, her new Mandarin exchange partner.

🔊 03.01 Since this is Lucy's first time meeting Jùnfēng, she needs to introduce herself. How does Lucy introduce herself to Jùnfēng?

Jùnfēng : Wèi … Nǐ hǎo.

Lucy : Nǐ hǎo, Jùnfēng. Wǒ jiào Lucy. Wǒ hěn **gāoxìng rènshi nǐ**.

Jùnfēng : Lucy, hěn gāoxìng rènshi nǐ. Nà … Wǒ yǒu diǎn jǐnzhāng.

Lucy : Wǒ yě shì!

Jùnfēng : Suǒyǐ … gàosu wǒ ba… nǐ yǒu shénme àihào?

Lucy : Duìbùqǐ, wǒ tīng bú dào… Qǐng zài shuō yíbiàn.

Jùnfēng : Méi wèntí. Xiànzài ne? Nǐ tīng de dào ma?

Lucy : Tīng de dào.

Jùnfēng : Hǎo. Nà, nǐ yǒu shénme àihào?

Lucy : Wǒ xǐhuan tīng yīnyuè. Wǒ yě xǐhuan lǚxíng. Nǐ ne?

Jùnfēng : Wǒ xǐhuan **wán** diànzǐ yóuxì, yě xǐhuan kànshū.

Lucy : Màn yìdiǎn. Shénme yóuxì?

Jùnfēng : Diànzǐ yóuxì.

FIGURE IT OUT

1 Use context to figure out which statement is false.

   a Lucy has trouble hearing Jùnfēng.

   b Jùnfēng wants to know what Lucy's hobbies are.

   c Lucy and Jùnfēng share the same hobbies.

2 How do you say 'no problem', 'so tell me', and 'sorry' in Chinese?

   a _____ _____

   b _____ _____

   c _____ _____

3 Highlight the phrases 'Can you hear?' and 'I can hear' in Chinese.

4 After Lucy mishears Jùnfēng, she says **Qǐng zài shuō yíbiàn**. Can you guess what this means in English?

   _____

   _____

NOTICE

🔊 **03.02** Listen to the audio and pay special attention to the pronunciation of **tīng bú dào**, **lǚxíng** and **Qǐng zài shuō yíbiàn**.

Essential phrases for Conversation 1

Chinese	Meaning	Literal translation
Wǒ jiào ...	My name is ...	I called ...
Wǒ yǒudiǎn jǐnzhāng.	I'm a little nervous.	I have a little nervous.
Wǒ yěshì!	Me too!	I also am!
Suǒyǐ ...	So ...	So ...
gàosu wǒ ba	so tell me	tell me [suggestion marker]
yǒu	to have	have
àihào	hobby	hobby
duìbùqǐ	sorry, excuse me	correct not polite
tīng bú dào	can't hear	hear not arrive
Qǐng zài shuō yíbiàn.	Please say it again.	Please again say one time.
méi wèntí	no problem	no problem
tīng de dào	can hear	hear of arrive
tīng yīnyuè	listen to music	hear music
lǚxíng	to travel	to travel
wán diànzǐ yóuxì	to play video games	to play electronic game
kànshū	to read	look book
màn yìdiǎn	please slow down	slow slow a little

GRAMMAR STRATEGY: *bù* vs *méi*

In the dialogue, you learned another word for not – **méi**. Wondering how it's different from **bù**? Simply put, **méi** has two main uses. The first is whenever the verb **yǒu** is negative. In other words, you wouldn't say **bù yǒu** but **méiyǒu**. If you remember **méiyǒu** as a set phrase, you won't need to worry about using the wrong negation.

The other use of **méi** is to negate something in the past. Here are a few examples of how the two negations compare:

Nǐ méi qù	You didn't go	**Nǐ bú qù**	You don't go
Wǒ méi chī zǎofàn.	I didn't eat breakfast.	**Wǒ bù chī zǎofàn.**	I don't eat breakfast.
Wǒ méi wèn tā.	I didn't ask him.	**Wǒ bú wèn tā.**	I don't ask him.

PRACTICE

1 What phrase can you use when someone is speaking too fast and you'd like them to slow down?

_____

_____

2 How do you ask 'What?' in Chinese?

_____

_____

3 Fill in the gaps to say in Chinese:

  a Nice to meet you.   **Wǒ hěn** _____ **rènshi nǐ**.

  b Please say it again.   _____ **zài shuō yíbiàn**.

  c How about now?   **Xiànzài** _____?

4 Write the English meaning of the Chinese verbs:

shuō	tīng	gàosu	yǒu	xǐhuan
a _____	b _____	c _____	d _____	e _____

CONVERSATION STRATEGY: learn set phrases

It's important to learn and use new phrases before you learn to understand the meaning of each individual word or the grammatical rationale behind them. For instance, you need to learn to say 'nice to meet you' way before you need to learn why Chinese uses the structure it does for that expression.

Learn these expressions now as set phrases – you'll use them all the time. We'll cover the hows and whys of them later on, when understanding the grammar behind them will help you expand your conversational abilities.

Wǒ hěn gāoxìng rènshi nǐ – a chunk that means 'nice to meet you'. Chinese don't say 'nice to meet' a person but 'happy to meet'!

Qǐng zài shuō yíbiàn. – how you say 'please say it again'!

1 Fill in the gaps with the correct question word: ma or ne. (In some cases both question words are possible).

a	So you like video games?	1	**Nǐ xǐhuan diànzǐ yóuxì _____?**
b	Do you like listening to music?	2	**Nǐ xǐhuan tīng yīnyuè _____?**
c	Can you hear?	3	**Nǐ tīng de dào _____?**
d	So then, you speak French?	4	**Nǐ huì shuō Fǎyǔ _____?**
e	Are you learning Chinese?	5	**Nǐ zhèngzài xuéxí Zhōngwén _____?**
f	So you're learning Chinese?	6	**Nǐ zhèngzài xuéxí Zhōngwén _____?**

2 Match the English question with its translation in Chinese.

a	What's your name?	1	**Nǐ tīng de dào ma?**
b	Where are you from?	2	**Nǐ míngbai le ma?**
c	Do you live in Beijing?	3	**Nǐ yǒu shénme àihào?**
d	What are your hobbies?	4	**Nǐ shì nǎli rén?**
e	Can you hear?	5	**Nǐ jiào shénme míngzi?**
f	Do you understand?	6	**Nǐ zhù zài Běijīng ma?**

3 Fill in the gaps with the missing word(s) in Chinese.

a **Wǒ _____ jǐnzhāng**. (I'm nervous.)

b **Màn _____.** (Please slow a bit.)

c **Nǐ yǒu _____ àihào?** (What are your hobbies?)

d **Wǒ _____ míngbai le.** (I understand now.)

GRAMMAR EXPLANATION: repeated verbs

In Chinese, you can duplicate the verb to soften your tone or to imply briefness. It also gives you a little extra time to work out what you'd like to say next.

Here are a few examples of verb duplication in action:

Nǐ kànkan.	Take a look.
Qǐng nǐ shuōshuo ba.	Please speak a bit.
Tīngting zhè shǒu gē.	Listen to this song.

Soften the following sentences by duplicating the verb.

1 **Nǐ wán ba!** (You may play!) _____ _____

2 **Qǐng xuéxí Zhōngwén.** (Please study Chinese) _____ _____

3 **Nǐ wèn.** (You ask.) _____ _____

PUT IT TOGETHER

1 Now write a few sentences about yourself in Chinese. Use your dictionary to look up new words you need, and try to answer the questions:

Nǐ jiào shénme míngzi?

_____

_____

Nǐ yǒu shénme àihào?

_____

_____

Nǐ bù xǐhuan shénme?

_____

_____

2 Imagine you are talking directly to a friend, what are some of the phrases you could use if you can't hear or don't understand? Use the phrases you've seen in this unit.

_____

_____

_____

_____

CONVERSATION 2

I don't understand

Lucy continues her online class, and Jùnfēng asks Lucy what kind of music she likes. She has trouble understanding Jùnfēng.

◀))) 03.03 How does Jùnfēng rephrase his sentences when Lucy asks for help?

> **Jùnfēng :** Nǐ xǐhuan jīngjù ma?
>
> **Lucy :** Duìbuqǐ. Wǒ bù míngbai.
>
> **Jùnfēng :** Nǐ xǐhuan shénme yīnyuè?
>
> **Lucy :** A, xiànzài míngbai le. Wǒ xǐhuan juéshìyuè, yě xǐhuan liúxíng yīnyuè.
>
> **Jùnfēng :** Zhēn de ma? Hěn yǒu yìsi.
>
> **Lucy :** Nǐ ne? Nǐ xǐhuan tīng shénme yīnyuè?
>
> **Jùnfēng :** Wǒ xǐhuan diànzǐ yīnyuè. Lǎoshí shuō, wǒ bù xǐhuan jīngjù.
>
> **Lucy :** Qǐng zài shuō yíbiàn. Nǐ bù xǐhuan shénme yīnyuè?
>
> **Jùnfēng :** Jīngjù. **Běijīng de gējù** … de yīnyuè. Míngbai le ma?
>
> **Lucy :** Qǐng děng yíxià. Hái tīng bú dào.

GRAMMAR TIP:
de (possession)
When showing possession, use _de_ to connect the possession to the possessor. In the dialogue, you saw **Běijīng de gējù**, or 'Beijing's opera'. A few more examples of how this is used are: **Lucy de shū** (Lucy's book), **wǒ de yīnyuè** (my music), or **nǐ de àihào** (your hobby).

BUILDING 'ME-SPECIFIC' LANGUAGE

In Unit 1, you learned the importance of building 'me-specific' vocabulary. Remember, when you meet a vocab list, don't try to memorize all the words – focus on the words you need in your own conversations.

Read the table below and add three of your own hobbies and interests.

Hobbies			
chànggē	singing	diànshì jiémù	TV show
tīzúqiú	playing football	diànyǐng	film
yóuyǒng	swimming	shū	book
kàn diànyǐng	watching films	yīnyuè	music
tiàowǔ	dancing	wǔshù	martial arts
dǎ bàngqiú	playing baseball	bókè	blog
dǎ lánqiú	playing basketball	zhàopiàn	photo
shèyǐng	photography	huà	painting (n)
_____	_____	_____	_____
_____	_____	_____	_____
_____	_____	_____	_____

FIGURE IT OUT

1 **Duì or cuò?** Select the correct answer.

   a Lucy asks Jùnfēng to repeat what he said.　　**duì** / **cuò**

   b Jùnfēng likes Beijing opera.　　**duì** / **cuò**

   c Lucy likes jazz and pop music.　　**duì** / **cuò**

2 Highlight the phrases in which:

   a Jùnfēng asks Lucy what kind of music she likes.

   b Jùnfēng says 'to be honest'.

3 What phrase does Jùnfēng use to express he finds Lucy's comment interesting? What word have you seen in this phrase to mean 'to have'?

4 What is the meaning of these phrases?

a Hái tīng bú dào.

b Nǐ bù xǐhuan shénme yīnyuè?

c Zhēn de ma?

5 Find one phrase in the conversation that you don't understand and use the context to infer its meaning. Look the phrase up online and check!

NOTICE

1 ◀) **03.04** Listen to the audio and study the table. Repeat the phrases to mimic the speaker. Pay special attention to the way the speaker pronounces the words:

Essential phrases for Conversation 2

Chinese	Meaning	Literal translation
jīngjù	Beijing Opera	Beijing Opera
juéshìyuè	jazz	jazz
liúxíng yīnyuè	pop music	popular music
Zhēn de ma?	Really?	true of [question marker]?
hěn yǒu yìsi	interesting	very have meaning
diànzǐ yīnyuè	electronic music	electronic music
gējù	opera	opera
lǎoshí shuō	to be honest	honest speak
děng yíxià	wait a moment	wait one moment

2 Notice how Lucy uses the Chinese word for 'a moment' to ask Jùnfēng to wait. Write out the missing words.

a Qǐng _____ yíxià. (Please listen a moment.)

b Qǐng _____ yíxià. (Please study a moment.)

c Wǒ xiǎng yào _____ yíxià. (I want to practice a moment.)

3 Use examples from the phrase lists and the language you know to translate each of the following.

   a You want to practice a moment.   _____ _____

   b I want to wait.   _____ _____

   c I want to live in Beijing.   _____ _____

   d Lucy wants to study Chinese.   _____ _____

   e Jùnfēng wants to play video games.   _____ _____

   f You want to listen to music.   _____ _____

4 Lucy uses several 'survival phrases' to tell Jùnfēng she's having trouble with her Chinese. Jùnfēng also uses one. Write them out in Chinese in the cheat sheet.

Survival phrases are your secret weapon for 'surviving' any conversation in Chinese, even when you're having trouble understanding. Learn these phrases, and you'll never have an excuse to switch back to English.

   a Sorry.

   b I don't understand.

   c Really?

   d Please say that again.

   e Please wait a moment.

   f I still don't understand.

 #LANGUAGEHACK: get a head start with words you already know

I've already introduced you to a few familiar words (or 'loanwords') in the past units.

When learning Chinese, it can feel like you're starting from scratch, especially when compared to European languages.

While it's true that most words you learn don't resemble English at all, you'd be surprised at how many Chinese words you recognize when you hear them spoken. As an English speaker, you know more words in Mandarin than you realize! With a few minutes' effort to get the tones right, you will be able to say them yourself without much mental effort.

How to guess English–Chinese loanwords

Country names

In many cases, especially for western countries, country names sound very similar to English. For instance:

> **Àiěrlán** (Ireland), **Yìdàlì** (Italy), **Bōlán** (Poland), **Jiānádà** (Canada), **Gēlúnbǐyà** (Colombia) and **Èguāduōěr** (Ecuador).
>
> The first syllable of many other countries has a similar sound to the country followed by 国 **guó** (which means 'country'):
>
> **Měiguó** (America), **Yīngguó** (England), **Déguó** (Germany /Deutschland) and **Fǎguó** (France).

Other loan words appear in:

> ## Brand names
> **Kěkǒukělè** (Coca-Cola), **Kǎdìyà** (Cartier) and **ài Fèng** (iPhone).
> ## The names of famous figures
> **Àiyīnsītǎn** (Einstein), **Línkěn** (Lincoln), **Dá'ěrwén** (Darwin), **Àohuā·Yúnfèi** (Oprah Winfrey) and **Àobāmǎ** (Obama).

> ## International foods
> Food dishes from other countries are often loan words in Chinese as well. There's **kāfēi** (coffee), **qiǎokèlì** (chocolate), **shālā** (salad), **péigēn** (bacon), **sānmíngzhì** (sandwich) and **gālí** (curry).

> ## Other recently borrowed words
> **Bàibài** (bye-bye), **bā** (bar), **bǐjīní** (bikini), **kǎlùlǐ** (calorie) and **pàiduì** (party).

YOUR TURN: use the hack

1 Match the Chinese names with their English equivalents.

a	Tāngmǔ · Hànkèsī	1	Brad Pitt
b	Bùlādé · Bǐtè	2	Angela Merkel
c	Wēilián · Shāshìbǐyǎ	3	Tom Hanks
d	Ānjílā · Mòkè'ěr	4	Jane Austin
e	Wēiěr · Shǐmìsī	5	William Shakespeare
f	Zhēnnífó · Láolúnsī	6	Will Smith
g	Jiǎn · Àosītīng	7	Jennifer Lawrence
h	Dàwèi · Bèikèhàmǔ	8	David Beckham

Wondering what · is? In Chinese, foreign names use this punctuation between the first and last name to help separate them when reading. Why? When Chinese is written using characters, there aren't any spaces! This dot helps make names clear.

CONVERSATION STRATEGY:
'Tarzan Mandarin'

As a beginner, you won't always know how to say exactly what you want to say. Instead of feeling frustrated, focus on getting your point across, rather than speaking eloquently. This means getting comfortable making mistakes.

That's why I recommend you embrace 'Tarzan Mandarin'. Find ways to convey your ideas that are understandable. You can still get your meaning across if you know just the key words.

For example, if you want to say 'Could you tell me where the bank is?' (**Qǐng gàosu wǒ yínháng zài nǎli?**) you could convey the same meaning with only two words, 'Bank ... where?' (**yínháng ... zài?**) Just like Tarzan!

Call the fear of making mistakes 'perfectionist paralysis'. Perfectionism is your enemy because it will hold you back from actually communicating. If you wait to say everything perfectly, you'll never say anything at all!

2 Try out your 'Tarzan Mandarin'. Look at these sentences and isolate the key words. Then use 'Tarzan Mandarin' to convey the same meaning!

Example: Duìbùqǐ, wǒ bù míngbai. Qǐng zài shuō yíbiàn. → Qǐng, yíbiàn.

a **Duìbùqǐ, qǐng màn yìdiǎn zài shuō yíbiàn.** (Sorry, can you say that again slowly.)

_____

_____

b **Qǐng gàosu wǒ, zhè ge duōshao qián?** (Can you please tell me how much this is?)

_____

_____

c **Qǐngwèn, nǐ zhīdao zhè ge zài nǎli ma?** (May I ask, do you know where this is?)

_____

_____

Mistakes are a necessary part of the process. In fact, they aren't just inevitable, they're important for making progress. In games like chess, players are advised to lose 50 games as soon as possible. Why not take this philosophy to the extreme and aim to make 200 mistakes a day in Chinese? Get them out of your system sooner, and you can improve so much faster.

PRACTICE

1 You've now seen several of the main question words used in Chinese! Fill in the cheat sheet.

> ### Question words cheat sheet
>
> | Meaning | Chinese | Meaning | Chinese |
> |---------|---------|---------|---------|
> | Why? | Wèitishénme? | Who? | Shéi? |
> | What? | _____ | How long? | Duōjiǔ? |
> | How? | Zěnme? | How much? | Duōshao? |
> | Where? | _____ | How is? | Zěnmeyàng? |
> | When? | Shénme shíhou? | | |

2 What question words would you ask in Chinese to get the following answers?

    a **Jīntiān** (today)   **d** **Zài Běijīng**

    b $2   **e** **Shū**

    c Lucy

3 Read the answers and select the correct question word.

    a **Nǐ wèishénme / duōjiǔ yào xuéxí Zhōngwén?** – **Wō xǐhuan yǔyán.**

    b **Nǐ yào shénme / shéi?** – **Wǒ de shū.**

    c **Nǐ shénme shíhou / wèishénme xuéxí?** – **Měitiān** (every day).

    d **Jùnfēng shì shéi / duōshao?** – **Wǒ de lǎoshī.**

    e **Nǐ zhù duōjiǔ / zài nǎli?** – **Wǒ zhù zài Měiguó.**

    f **Nǐ de pīsà zěnmeyàng / wèishénme?** – **Hǎo.**

4 Combine words you know to create new sentences in Chinese.

    a Where do you live? **Nǐ zhù** _____?

    b What are you saying? **Nǐ shuō** _____?

    c Why do you want to live in Beijing? **Nǐ** _____ **yào zhù zài Běijīng?**

    d How is your book? **Nǐ de shū,** _____?

    e What do you want to listen to? **Nǐ yào tīng** _____?

GRAMMAR EXPLANATION: 'le' – the past tense?

The Chinese marker **le** is often described as the past tense marker, but this isn't completely true. The marker **le** indicates a change of state, as well as a few other things – but we'll leave those for later.

Example: Wǒ míngbai le.

In this example, the **le** implies that the sentence means 'I understand now, but I didn't before.' The change of state is that there is an understanding that wasn't there in the past.

Example: Nǐ huì shuō Zhōngwén le.

This sentence means 'you can speak Chinese now', implying that you didn't have the ability to speak Mandarin in the past.

1 🔊 **03.05** Can you guess how to say the following phrases in Mandarin? Write them out below, then listen to the audio to check your answers.

a I study French (but didn't in the past).

_____

_____

b Everyday, I practice (but didn't in the past).

_____

_____

c I like Beijing opera (but didn't in the past).

_____

_____

PUT IT TOGETHER

Use what you've learned in Conversations 1 and 2, as well as new 'me-specific' vocab you looked up in your dictionary, to create new sentences about yourself in Chinese. Be sure to include:

⋯⟩ what your hobbies are
⋯⟩ what you don't like to do
⋯⟩ what kind of music you like listening to
⋯⟩ what kind of music you don't like.

UNDERSTANDING PINYIN: THE FINAL SOUNDS

In the two previous units, you learned the consonants that form the initials in the pinyin system. In this section, you'll learn the finals.

Finals are primarily composed of vowels, though there are a few exceptions. Get started below.

1 🔊 **03.06** Here are the sounds. Listen to the audio and study the table.

a	(like awesome)	er	(like dirt)
e	(like ugly)	ia	(like yard)
i	(like me)	ie	(like yes)
o	(like row)	iu	(like you)
u	(like ooh)	iao	(like meow)
ü	(like ew)	ian	(like lan)
ai	(like eye)	in	(like in)
ei	(like hey)	ua	(like watch)
ao	(like ow)	uo	(like woah)
ou	(like mow)	uai	(like why)
an	(like ant)	ui	(like way)
en	(like when)	uan	(like want)
ang	(like long)	un	(like moon)
eng	(like mung)		

2 🔊 **03.07** Listen to the audio and write the final sound you hear.

a _____	g _____	l _____	s _____
b _____	h _____	m _____	t _____
c _____	i _____	n _____	u _____
d _____	j _____	o _____	v _____
e _____	k _____	p _____	w _____
f _____		q _____	x _____
		r _____	

MORE CHINESE CHARACTERS

'Me', 'you', 'he' and 'she' – these are all words you'll use, hear, see and
read often in Chinese. Learning to recognize these characters will help
improve your reading comprehension and set you on the path to writing
your 'me-specific' sentences.

我 wǒ

The character for 'I' in Chinese is 我. It is a combination of the radical 手
shǒu meaning 'hand' and 戈 gē meaning 'spear'. It has historical origins
in the sense that it is derived from 'I am holding my spear' in my hand.
It may look slightly intimidating at first, but once you start practicing,
you'll quickly get the hang of it.

This character has seven strokes. They are drawn in the following order:

我 wǒ
7 strokes

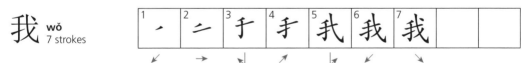

Practice writing this character in the space below.

你 nǐ

The Chinese character for 'you' is made up of the radical 人 (man), written as 亻 when on the left, and 尔 ěr (thou) on the right.

The left radical is written first, then the part on the right is written.

'You' also has seven strokes. They are written in this order:

你 nǐ
(7 strokes)

Practice writing this character in the space below:

他 tā

The character for 'he' also has the radical 人 (man) on the left. 也 (also) on the right suggests that 'he is also a person'.

The character for 'he' is written with five strokes. They are written in this order:

他 tā
(5 strokes)

Practice writing this character in the space below:

她 tā

The last character you'll learn in this unit is the character for 'she' in Chinese. It looks very similar to the character for 'he' but the left component, or radical, is different. It's the radical for 'woman' 女.

It's pronounced in the exact same way as 'him', so you only need to remember one word when you're speaking!

The character for 'she' is written in six strokes. They are drawn in this order:

她 tā
(6 strokes)

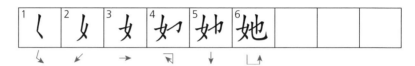

Practice writing this character in the space below:

COMPLETING UNIT 3

Check your understanding

🔊 **03.08** Review the conversations from this unit, and when you're feeling confident:

···⟩ listen to the audio and write down what you hear
···⟩ and feel free to pause or replay the audio as often as you need.

This exercise gives you a chance to practice your listening skills, which is very important. But remember – this isn't a school exam! Judge your results based on how well you're able to understand the audio, rather than whether you spell everything perfectly.

Show what you know ...

Here's what you've just learned. Write or say an example for each item in the list. Then check off the ones you know.

- ☐ Say 'nice to meet you' without using **wǒ** and 'my name is'.
- ☐ Say 'I like' and 'I don't like'.
- ☐ Say something that you like to do and something that you don't like to do.
- ☐ Use the survival phrases, 'Say that again', 'I didn't hear' and 'Slower, please'.
- ☐ Use the question words When?, Where?, Why?, How? and Who?
- ☐ Use the Chinese words for the kinds of music that you like and don't like. Use your dictionary if you don't know the word for your favorite genre!

COMPLETE YOUR MISSION

It's time to complete your mission using 'Tarzan Mandarin' to play (and win!) the word game. To do this, you'll need to prepare phrases for describing a Mandarin-speaking person, place or thing that other people could guess – without knowing the word itself.

STEP 1: build your script

Let's embrace 'imperfectionism' with today's script. Highlight the key words you need to convey your point, then look them up in your dictionary – but don't try to have perfect grammar! If you come across a complex expression, try to think of simpler words to convey the same idea.

If you get stuck, you're probably struggling with perfectionist paralysis. Take a step back and remind yourself that your script is supposed to be imperfect today!

Keep building your script using 'Tarzan Mandarin' and the unit conversation strategies. Be sure to:

⋯⟩ describe a famous person
⋯⟩ for that person, describe him / her with any words you know (What is his/her nationality? What are his/her hobbies?)

Share what they're famous for: **diànyǐng** (a film), **yì shǒu gē** (a song), **yìshù** (art)

For example, you could say:

Yīngguó rén ... chúshī (chef) ... **chángcháng shēngqì** (often angry) ... **yǒu diànshì jiémù** (has a TV show)

You may need to look up a few new words to complete this activity. Write down your script, then repeat it until you feel confident.

STEP 2: practice makes perfect ... online

Getting over the embarrassment of 'sounding silly' is part of language learning. Use your 'Tarzan Mandarin' to help you overcome these fears! Upload your clip to the community area, and you'll be surprised at how much encouragement you'll get.

It's time to complete your mission and share a recording with the community. Go online to find your mission for Unit 3 and see how far you can get with your 'Tarzan Mandarin'.

STEP 3: learn from other learners

Can you guess the words? After you've uploaded your own clip, get inspiration from how others use 'Tarzan Mandarin'. Your task is to play the game and try to guess the words other people describe. Take note of the clever ways they use the conversation strategies from the unit and stash them away as a mental note to try later on your own.

STEP 4: reflect on what you learned

Did you learn about new places and people from the community? Write down anything interesting that you might want to look into later – a famous actor you might want to look up, or a film you may want to see. What gaps did you identify in your own language when doing your mission? What words do you reach for over and over? Are there any words you hear frequently, but don't understand? Keep note of them!

Really! The more time you spend on a task, the better you will get! (Studies show that you will be 30% better than your peers who don't practice their speaking regularly.)

HACK IT: change your search preferences to 中文 (Zhōngwén)
Did you know that many major websites automatically detect your language from your browser settings, and adjust accordingly? You can change these settings to 中文, and you'll instantly notice your search engine, social networking sites and video searches will automatically change to Chinese!

You can also simply go to google.cn to search Chinese language websites around the world – then be sure to type your keywords in Chinese!

HEY, LANGUAGE HACKER, DO YOU REALIZE HOW MUCH YOU CAN ALREADY SAY?

By learning to work around a limited vocab, you really can start speaking Mandarin with other people in no time. It's not about learning all the words and grammar. It's about communicating – sometimes creatively. By finishing this mission, you've learned valuable skills that you'll use again and again in the real world.

Next, you'll learn to talk about your plans for the future.

Jiāyóu!

4 TALKING ABOUT FRIENDS AND FAMILY

Mission

Imagine this – you're chatting with someone you met at a local language group about your family and friends and realize you may have a friend in common!

Your mission is to describe the person and their relationship to you, where they live and work, and who their siblings, parents and/or children are, in order to confirm if in fact it's a common friend.

This mission will get you comfortable talking about your family and friends using new verb forms as well as descriptive language.

Mission prep

⋯⟩ Use 'you plural', 'we', and 'they'.
⋯⟩ Learn essential family vocabulary.
⋯⟩ Use phrases to describe things you plan to do with other people: **gēn ... yìqǐ**.
⋯⟩ Learn four new Chinese characters.

BUILDING LANGUAGE FOR TALKING ABOUT SOMEONE ELSE

Until now, our conversations have focused on describing **wǒ** and **nǐ**. We'll build on that now with vocab you can use to talk about anyone else.

#LANGUAGEHACK
use clues and context to understand much more than you think

CONVERSATION 1

Do you have any siblings?

GRAMMAR TIP:

men

To make nouns related to humans plural, you add **men**. This doesn't apply to non-human nouns like objects or animals! So for the pronoun 'you' to become 'you all' nǐ becomes **nǐmen**. 'I' becomes 'we' in **wǒmen** and 'he' or 'she' becomes 'they' in **tāmen**. For example, you could say **péngyoumen** for 'friends' or **sì ge péngyou** for 'four friends', but not **sì ge péngyoumen**.

Lucy is back at her local language group. Today she is getting to know Xiǎowēi better, and is building up her confidence in delving into new conversation topics. They both talk about their siblings.

🔊 **04.01** Lucy has a younger brother David and a younger sister Ann. Read or listen carefully to the conversation and try to figure out the words for 'younger brother' and 'younger sister'.

Xiǎowēi : Lucy nǐ hǎo! Nǐ zuìjìn zěnmeyàng?

Lucy : Wǒ hěn hǎo. Nǐ ne?

Xiǎowēi : Wǒ yě hǎo. Shàng ge zhōumò wǒ hé wǒ de gēge chūqù wán le.

Lucy : Tài hǎo le. Tā jiào shénme míngzi?

Xiǎowēi : Tā jiào Lǐwèi. Tā hé tā de qīzi zhù zài Tiānjīn. Nǐ yǒu xiōngdì jiěmèi ma?

Lucy : Wǒ yǒu yí ge mèimei, yí ge dìdi.

Xiǎowēi : Tā **men** jiào shénme míngzi?

Lucy : Wǒ de dìdi jiào David. Wǒ de mèimei jiào Ann. David gēn wǒ de fùmǔ zhù zài yìqǐ.

Xiǎowēi : Nǐ jiéhūn le ma?

Lucy : Méiyou. Dànshì Ann, wǒ de mèimei yǐjing...**ēn**... jiéhūn le. Tā yǒu **liǎng ge háizi**. Yí ge nǚhái hé yí ge nánhái.

Xiǎowēi : Wǒ de gēge yě yǒu háizi.

CONVERSATION STRATEGY: the 'Captain Jack Sparrow' technique

Hesitation is unavoidable when you start learning a new language. Filler words can make things smoother, but another good option is to summon your inner Captain Jack Sparrow! When you start a sentence and need to gather your thoughts, don't just hesitate – pause – as if you're deep in thought. Hesitating with confidence makes it seem you're about to say something extremely interesting – even if you're just describing your day!

VOCABULARY: two

In Chinese, there are two words for the word 'two'. You already learned **èr**, the number used for counting or numbers (such as telling the time or ordinal numbers like 'second'). **Liǎng** is used with measure words. Use this word whenever you want to say there are two of something, as in **liǎng ge háizi** or **liǎng běn shū**. Don't worry if you use the wrong one for now. You'll still be understood!

FIGURE IT OUT

1 What are the words for 'siblings' that appear in the dialogue?

    a older brother _____

    b siblings (lit. brothers sisters) _____

    c younger brother _____

    d younger sister _____

2 Find and highlight the Chinese phrases:

    a You know the phrase for 'What is your name?'. Look at the dialogue and find where Lucy asks, 'What is his name?'

        _____

        _____

    b Write down the phrase Xiǎowēi uses to say, 'His name is …'

        _____

        _____

    c Find where Xiǎowēi asks Lucy, 'Do you have siblings?'

        _____

        _____

    d How do you say '… lives with my parents'? Hint: Lucy uses this phrase to talk about her brother David.

        _____

        _____

    e Xiǎowēi asks Lucy if she is married, and Lucy responds that she isn't but her sister Ann is. What's the Chinese word for 'married'?

        _____

        _____

3 The following statements about the conversation are **cuò**. Review the dialogue and highlight the incorrect part of the statements below, then write the correct phrase in Mandarin.

    a **Lǐwèi zhù zài Guǎngzhōu**. (Lǐwèi lives in Guangzhou.)

        _____

        _____

b Ann gēn wǒ de fùmǔ zhù zài yìqǐ. (Ann lives with Lucy's parents.)

_____

_____

c Lǐwèi méiyǒu háizi. (Lǐwèi doesn't have children.)

_____

_____

d Xià ge zhōumò Xiǎowēi hé gēge chūqù wán. (Xiǎowēi is going to hang out with her brother next weekend.)

_____

_____

4 You've learned a lot of words that tell you when something is happening. Find the following words in brackets and write their Mandarin translations.

a _____ **wǒ hé wǒ de dìdi chūqù wán le.** (last weekend)

b **Nǐ** _____ **zěnmeyàng?** (lately)

c **A,** _____ **míngbai le.** (now) Hint: refer to Unit 3 if you need help remembering this one!

d _____ **wǒ yào liànxí yíxià.** (today) Hint: you learned this one in Unit 2!

e **Wǒ de mèimei** _____ **ēn ... jiéhūn le.** (already)

5 Lucy shares that her sister has two children. Find the phrase she uses to share this information and write it below.

_____

_____

NOTICE

🔊 **04.02** Listen to the audio and study the table. Repeat the phrases to mimic the speakers.

Essential phrases for Conversation 1

Chinese	Meaning	Literal translation
Nǐ zuìjìn zěnmeyàng?	How have you been lately?	You lately how about?
shàng ge zhōumò	last weekend	above [measure word] weekend
dìdi	younger brother	younger brother
chūqù wán le	hung out	go out play [change marker]
Tā jiào shénme míngzi?	What is his/her name?	He/she called what name?
qīzi	wife	wife
Nǐ yǒu xiōngdì jiěmèi ma?	Do you have any siblings?	You have brothers sisters [question marker]?
yí ge	one [measure word]	one [measure word]
gēge	older brother	older brother
mèimei	younger sister	younger sister
tāmen	they	he/she [plural]
gēn	with	with
fùmǔ	parents	father mother
yìqǐ	together	together
yǐjing	already	already
ēn	umm	umm
jiéhūn	married	married
liǎng	two	two
háizi	child	child
nǚhái	girl	female child
nánhái	boy	male child
dànshì	but	but

GRAMMAR TIP: ge

In Unit 2, you were introduced to measure words when you learned about time – **sì ge xīngqī** (four weeks) and **sì ge yuè** (four months). Chinese uses different measure words to classify different things. For example, **zhī** is the measure word for many animals and body parts – **liǎng zhī gǒu** (two dogs) or **wǔ zhī shǒu** (five hands). **Tiáo** is the measure word for long, wavy objects like belts, rivers or fish – **sì tiáo yú** (four fish). If you ever forget which measure word to use, the world will not end. So, don't worry! You can almost always use **ge** and still be understood.

1 Write out the new phrases you can use to talk about your family with someone else:

a My younger sister lives with my parents.

_____

_____

b My older brother is married.

_____

_____

c I don't have a younger brother.

_____

_____

d I live with my brothers.

_____

_____

2 This conversation introduces forms for talking about 'he' and 'she' in Chinese. You'll also see a new word for 'they' and 'you plural'. Write out each of the following words in Chinese:

a he _____   **b** she _____   **c** they _____

d you _____   **e** you (plural) _____   **f** we _____

3 Use the examples to translate the English sentences.

a **Nǐ yǒu yí ge jiějie**. (You have an older sister.)

(You don't have an older sister.) _____

_____

b **Wǒ shì dìdi**. (I am the younger brother.)

(I am not the younger brother.) _____

_____

c **Wǒ yǒu liǎng ge jiěmèi**. (I have two sisters.)

(I have two brothers.) _____

_____

d **Tā gēn wǒ de fùmǔ zhù zài yìqǐ.** (He lives with my parents.)

(He lives with my younger sister.) _____

_____

e **Wǒ yǒu yí ge jiějie, dànshì wǒ méiyǒu mèimei.** (I have an older sister, but I don't have a younger sister.)

(I have a younger brother, but I don't have an older brother.) _____

_____

GRAMMAR EXPLANATION: gēn ... yìqǐ

To say that you do something with someone, you use **gēn ... yìqǐ**. This structure always comes before the verb – what's being done with the other person. In English, **gēn** means 'with' and **yìqǐ** means 'together', so you're literally saying 'together with'. The person you're doing something with goes between **gēn** and **yìqǐ**.

Let's look at a few examples.

Wǒ gēn yí ge péngyou yìqǐ qù xuéxiào. (I go to school with a friend.)

Nǐ yào gēn wǒ yìqǐ qù ma? (Do you want to go with me?)

Translate the following into Chinese:

a with my parents _____ _____

b with her older sister _____ _____

c with a friend _____ _____

d with his wife _____ _____

You'll often see **hé** (and) used in place of 'with'. So, 'he goes with my parents' could be either: **Tā gēn wǒ de fùmǔ yìqǐ qù** or **tā hé wǒ de fùmǔ yìqǐ qù.**

PRACTICE

Here's some new vocab you can use to talk about your family.

🔊 04.03 Listen to the audio and follow along with the table. Repeat the words as you hear them.

Chinese	Meaning	Chinese	Meaning
fùmǔ	parents	érzi / nǚ'ér	son / daughter
mǔqīn / fùqīn	mother / father	háizi	children
māma / bàba	mom / dad	yéye / nǎinai	paternal grandfather / grandmother
jiějie / gēge	older sister / older brother	wàigōng / wàipó	maternal grandfather / grandmother
mèimei / dìdi	younger sister / younger brother	qīzi / zhàngfu	wife / husband
xiōngdì jiěmèi	siblings (lit. brothers sisters)	péngyou / nánpéngyou / nǚpéngyou	friend / boyfriend / girlfriend
nánhái / nǚhái	boy / girl	āyí / shūshu	aunt / uncle
māo	cat	gǒu	dog
_____	_____	_____	_____
_____	_____	_____	_____

2 Use your dictionary to fill in the last two rows of the family members table with words for family members (or pets!) close to you, or other phrases to describe your personal situation.

3 Fill in the gaps with the missing words in Chinese.

   a **Nǐ yǒu** _____ **ma?** (Do you have any brothers?)

   b **Tā shì wǒ de** _____ (He is my son.)

   c **Wǒ de** _____ **hé wǒ yìqǐ chūqù wán le**. (My friend and I hung out together.)

   d **Wǒ** _____ **shì yīshēng**. (My mom is a doctor.)

   e **Nǐ de** _____ **zhù zài nǎli?** (Where do your parents live?)

4 Use the phrase list from Conversation 1 to answer the questions and practice creating sentences about someone close to you.

Example: Nǐ rènshi nǐ de péngyou duōjiǔ le? (How long have you known your friend?)

Wǒ rènshi tā sān nián le.

a　Nǐ rènshi nǐ de péngyou duōjiǔ le? _____

　　_____

b　Tā jiào shénme míngzi? _____ _____

c　Tā yǒu shénme àihào? _____ _____

d　Tā shì nǎguó rén? _____ _____

VOCABULARY EXPLANATION: aunt and uncle

Depending on how your aunt or uncle are related to you, you'll use a different word. This means your dad's older sister and your dad's younger sister each have a different word you use to refer to them. Your dad's brother's wife also has a unique word. As do your mother's siblings.

All of these words for 'aunt' and 'uncle' can get overwhelming, so you can use the more generic **āyí** and **shūshu** to get your point across. These literally mean 'dad's younger brother' for 'uncle' and 'mother's younger sister' for 'aunt', but they can be used to describe or to refer to a man or woman a generation older than you – even if they aren't a relative!

When you add **wǒ de** (my), it becomes clear that you're referring to your aunt and not someone else's.

When all else fails, you can use circumlocution to get your point across. So, to refer to your dad's younger brother, you can say **wǒ de bàba de dìdi** and for your mom's older brother's wife, **wǒ de māma de gēge de qīzi**.

You can also do the same for other extended family members. Try a few with circumlocution!

a　Your mother's older sister's daughter (cousin) _____

　　_____

b　Your father's father (grandfather) _____ _____

c　Your mother's father's older brother (great uncle) _____

　　_____

You might be tempted to talk about where you 'met' someone, but we haven't learned how to talk about things that happened (past tense) yet. It's coming up in Unit 7. In the meantime, practice rephrasing sentences so you can convey the same idea with what you know now. This is an invaluable skill in language learning.

PUT IT TOGETHER

1 Look up the 'me-specific' verbs you need to talk about the people close to you, then write at least three sentences to talk about:

where you or members of your family live.

Example: Wǒ zhù zài ..., wǒ de jiārén (family) ...

what some friends or family members like to do.

Example: Wǒ xǐhuan ..., Thomas ...

_____

_____

_____

2 Who is your favorite person? Who do you spend your time with? Use your dictionary and new vocab to write out details like:

···⟩ What is his/her name? Where does he/she live?

···⟩ Who does he/she live with? (e.g. **gēn** Peter)

···⟩ What does he/she like to do?

CONVERSATION 2

What do you have planned?

Lucy has been taking online Chinese classes for a few weeks. Today she's
practicing with Jùnfēng, and she's excited to talk about the new friend
she's been getting to know at her language group.

🔊 04.04 Listen to how Lucy describes her plans with Xiǎowēi.

Jùnfēng : Wéi, Lucy. Nǐ hái hǎo ma?

Lucy : Hái hǎo. Xièxie. Zhè ge xīngqī wǒ yào hé yí ge xīn péngyou chūqù wán.

Jùnfēng : Tài bàng le. Tā shì shéi? Tā jiào shénme míngzi?

Lucy : Tā jiào Xiǎowēi. Tā shì gōngchéngshī. Tā zhù zài Běijīng, dànshì tā de jiārén
xiànzài zhù zài Tiānjīn.

Jùnfēng : Nǐmen yào zuò shénme?

Lucy : Míngtiān wǒmen qù Yíhéyuán wán. Zhè ge xīngqī nèi, wǒmen qù chénglǐ
kànkan. Wǒmen yào chángchang Běijīng kǎoyā. Xià ge xīngqī wǒmen qù
Tiānjīn kàn tā de jiārén.

Jùnfēng : Hěn yǒu yìsi. Wǒ de nǚpéngyou shì Tiānjīn rén. Měi nián Chūnjié tā dōu qù
Tiānjīn. Nǐmen qù kàn Chángchéng ma?

Lucy : Wǒ xiǎng qù. Wǒ yě xiǎng qù Gùgōng, kěnéng hái qù Wángfǔjǐng yèshì.

Jùnfēng : Dāngrán xūyào qù Wángfǔjǐng yèshì. Yǒu hěn duō hǎochī de dōngxi.

FIGURE IT OUT

1 Add the missing word to complete the following sentences:

   a _____ **chūqù wán**. (We are going to hang out.)

   b **Tā de jiārén xiànzài** _____ **Tiānjīn.** (Her family lives in Tianjin.)

   c **Nǐmen** _____ **zuò shénme?** (What do you all want to do?)

2 Answer the questions about the conversation. The bold sections of the questions will help you find the answers in the dialogue.

   a Lucy hé **shéi** chūqù wán?

   _____
   _____

   b Míngtiān tāmen qù **nǎli** wán?

   _____
   _____

   c Lucy yào chángchang **shénme?**

   _____
   _____

   d Jùnfēng de nǚpéngyou shì **nǎguó** rén?

   _____
   _____

NOTICE

🔊 **04.05** Listen to the audio and study the table.

Essential phrases for Conversation 2

Chinese	Meaning	Literal translation
Nǐ hái hǎo ma?	Are you well?	You still good [question marker]?
xièxie	thanks	thanks
xīn	new	new
gōngchéngshī	engineer	engineer
jiārén	family	house person
Nǐmen yào zuò shénme?	What do you want to do?	You [plural] want do what?
míngtiān	tomorrow	tomorrow
Yíhéyuán	Summer Palace	Summer Palace
zhè ge xīngqī nèi	during the week	this week inside
chéngshì	city	city
xiǎng	would like	would like
chángchang	to taste/to try	taste taste
Běijīng kǎoyā	Beijing duck	Beijing duck
xià ge xīngqī	next week	below [measure word] week
měi	every	every
chūnjié	Spring Festival	Spring Festival
Chángchéng	Great Wall	Great Wall
Gùgōng	Forbidden City	Forbidden City
kěnéng	maybe	maybe
Wángfǔjǐng yèshì	Wangfujing Night Market	Wangfujing Night Market
dāngrán	of course	of course
hěn duō hǎochī de dōngxi	lots of tasty things	very many good eat of things

VOCABULARY: *it's all in a week's work*
In this unit, you're learning that Chinese uses two words to say a few things pretty regularly! But we do this in English as well, so it's important to learn common synonyms (words that mean the same thing). You might say 'a pair' or 'a couple' and, similarly, 'happy' or 'glad'. In Chinese, another word you'll commonly see two versions of is 'week'. These are **xīngqī** as in Conversation 2 and **zhōu**. You'll frequently see and hear both, so becoming familiar with them is a good way to get a head start.

1 Find these words in the conversation and write them here.

a thanks _____ **b** but _____ **c** to do _____

d family _____ **e** girlfriend _____ **f** to see _____

2 How do you say these phrases in Chinese?

a my new friend _____

b this week _____

c during the week _____

d maybe _____

e of course you need to _____

3 Write the correct words to complete the sentences.

a **Tā jiào shénme** _____? (What is her name?)

b **Nǐmen yào** _____ **shénme?** (What do you want to do?)

c _____ **wǒmen qù Shànghǎi.** (Tomorrow we are going to Shanghai.)

d **Wǒ** _____ **rènshi tā.** (I maybe know her.)

e **Tā** _____ **kàn diànyǐng ma?** (He would like to see a movie?)

GRAMMAR TIP:
jǐ ge
Earlier, you learned that 'how many' is **duōshao** but here **jǐ ge** is used. What's the difference? **Jǐ ge** is used when there is a measure word and when there is an uncertain number under ten. **Duōshao** is used with any number, above or below ten, as well as when the measure word is omitted. **Nǐ yǒu jǐ ge mèimei?** (How many younger sisters do you have?) **Nǐ yǒu duōshao shū?** (How many books do you have? [assumes this is over 10])

PRACTICE

1 Practice answering questions about your relationships with other people.

a **Nǐ yǒu xiōngdì jiěmèi ma?** (Do you have siblings?) **Nǐ yǒu jǐ ge xiōngdì jiěmèi?** (How many siblings do you have?)

Yǒu / méiyǒu, (wǒ yǒu xiōngdì jiěmèi.)

b **Nǐ yǒu qīzi / zhàngfu ma?** (Do you have a husband / wife?) **Nǐ yǒu nánpéngyou / nǚpéngyou ma?** (Do do you have a boyfriend / girlfriend?)

Yǒu / méiyǒu...

c **Nǐ yǒu háizi ma? Jǐ ge?** (Do you have children? How many?)

Yǒu / méiyǒu, wǒ...

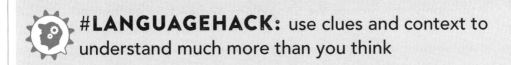

#LANGUAGEHACK: use clues and context to understand much more than you think

Getting into Chinese can feel overwhelming when you think there are so many words and sentence structures you don't know yet. But even as an absolute beginner, you have a huge head start. Here are four strategies you can use to help you understand when you are spoken to in Mandarin, even when a dictionary is nowhere in sight:

1 Get clues from the theme of the conversation

It's highly unlikely that you'll find yourself in a Mandarin conversation where you have no idea what the subject is. You can tune your ear to listen for particular themes – like hobby or interest words – **tǐyù** (sports), **yīnyuè**, **pēngrèn** (cooking), etc. – that give you clues to what other people might be saying, even if you're not able to understand most of the words.

Simply knowing what word category to expect can make a huge difference. For instance, if you aren't sure whether a person said **shū** (book) or **shù** (tree), then the fact that you're talking in a library should make it obvious!

A conversation is almost never about 'nothing'. There are topics people are more likely to discuss in a given conversation.

2 Use visual markers to infer meaning

Suppose you're at a restaurant on your first day in China, the waiter arrives and you hear '&%$## @@[]ç/&?'.

If you pay attention to the additional context you're getting from visual markers, then you can infer the meaning of new words and phrases.

Where is the person looking? Is the waiter looking at your glass?

Where are their hands or body pointing?

What facial expression do they have? What kind of reply is he looking for from you? Is he looking to see if you're satisfied? Or is he waiting for some specific information from you?

As well as visual markers, intonation will also tell you whether something is a question, a request, a command or a casual comment.

3 Look for signpost words at the beginnings and ends of sentences

The same way that you'll see signs alerting you when you're entering or leaving certain areas, conversations often work the same way. For instance, if you hear phrases along the lines of:

Shǒujī ... zài nǎli (Cellphone ... where), **Zuìjìn ... yīnyuè** (Recently ... music) or

xīngqī wǔ ... diànyǐngyuàn (Friday ... cinema), you can get a pretty good idea of the gist of the phrase as a whole. Each word brings you closer to the truth – even if you only recognize the beginning and ends!

Some common signpost words to look out for are:

> question words: **shéi, shénme shíhou, zài nǎli** (who, when, where)
>
> time indicators: **zhè ge xīngqī, chángcháng** (this week, usually)
>
> booster verbs: **Nǐ xiǎng ma? Kěyǐ ma?** (Would you like? Can I?).

4 Rely on connector words for hints to what's next.

Use the following connector prompts to create your own sentences in Chinese.

Rúguǒ nǐ xiǎng qù ... (If you would like to go ...) _____ _____

Wǒ hē kāfēi jiā niúnǎi, dànshì qǐng bù jiā ... (I like my coffee with milk but please don't add ...)

Connector words function to connect one part of a sentence with another, which makes them very reliable signposts for what type of information is to come!

In the examples, **dànshì qǐng bù jiā** is a big hint that the speaker doesn't like coffee with sugar, and **rúguǒ** most likely indicates a threat of some consequence. When you hear these words you can confidently infer that:

dànshì: there's contradiction of what was previously said. If you understood either statement, you can guess the other is opposing in some way.

rúguǒ: something unsure may happen, and you may hear a positive / negative consequence of it.

ránhòu (then): the first statement happened as a result of the second.

YOUR TURN: use the Hack

1 🔊 **04.06** Listen to the audio and try to figure out the 'theme' the person might be talking about. In the text below, highlight any keywords that give you clues to the theme.

    a Wǒ xiǎng mǎi yì tái xīn diànnǎo. Wǒ de diànnǎo huài le. Wǒ yǐjing yòng le liù nián le.

        Theme: _____

    b Míngnián wǒ qù Àodàliyà. Wǒ huì qù kàn yí ge péngyou. Tā zhù zài Xīní.

        Theme: _____

    c Wǒ jīntiān hé māma shuōhuá le. Tā shuō wǒ de gēge yǒu yí ge xīn de nǚpéngyou. Tāmen yǐjing xiǎng jiéhūn le.

        Theme: _____

    d Wǒ xué Xībānyáyǔ xué le yí ge yuè le. Wǒ kàn le hěnduō Xībānyá diànyǐng. Dànshì wǒ hái méiyǒu lǎoshī.

        Theme: _____

2 🔊 **04.07** Listen to the audio, and use signpost words or connector words to guess what sentence you think will follow.

    a [Xuéxí Zhōngwén yǐhòu]... wǒ yào xuéxí Déyǔ / ... wǒ huì xuéxí Déyǔ.

    b [Jīntiān wǒ gēn wǒ de péngyou]... tiānqì (weather) bù hǎo. / ... dǎ lánqiú.

    c [Wǒ yǒu yí ge jiějie dànshì]... wǒ xǐhuan kàn diànyǐng. / ... méiyǒu gēge.

3 Describe plans you have for a weekend together with a family member or friend. Refer back to the list of hobbies from Unit 3 and practice using these phrases:

wǒmen xiǎng ...   **wǒmen qù ...**

Example:

Zhè zhōumò wǒ gēn wǒ de gēge yìqǐ chūqù wán. Wǒmen qù kàn diànyǐng. Kàn diànyǐng yǐhòu, wǒmen qù yèshì chīfàn. (This weekend, I'm going to hang out with my older brother. We are going to see a movie. After seeing the movie, we are going to the night market to eat.)

PUT IT TOGETHER

Create a script of at least four sentences that's true for you about:

⋯❯ your parents or family – their names, hobbies or where they live
⋯❯ your children or siblings – their names, what they're doing or what they like
⋯❯ your friends – how long you've known them for, what they do or what they like
⋯❯ your co-workers – what they usually say
⋯❯ your pets, people you admire or anyone else you want to talk about!

You should now have most of the 'me-specific' vocab you need to talk about your family or group of friends!

MORE CHINESE CHARACTERS

Above and below, previous and next. Girlfriend and boyfriend, girl and boy. These are two sets of opposites with four words you've learned, and they lead into the next characters you'll learn.

上 shàng

The character for 'above' in Chinese is 上. 上 resembles a tree growing upward from the ground (the horizontal line) with a single branch. You can remember its meaning by the small line above the 'ground'.

The three strokes are drawn in the following order:

上 **shàng**
(3 strokes)

Practice writing this character in the space below.

下 xià

The Chinese character for 'below' is easy to remember because it has a
stroke drawn below the top stroke, much like 'above' has a stroke above
the bottom stroke. 下 resembles tree roots growing down from the
surface to seek water.

The three strokes are written in this order:

下 xià
(3 strokes)

Practice writing this character in the space below.

女 nǚ

The character for 'female' is an important character to learn because it's
used both as a character on its own and as a component of several other
characters, one of which you've already learned 她. You'll also see it in
妈妈 (mom), 姐姐 (older sister) and 妹妹 (younger sister). Since you've
learned these words in this unit, you'll know how the characters are
pronounced!

女 resembles the side view of a woman caring for her baby.

You can combine this character with another you've learned to get the word for 'woman' – 女人.

The three strokes are written in this order:

 nǚ
(3 strokes)

Practice writing this character in the space below.

男 nán

The last character you'll learn in this unit is the character for 'male' in Chinese. 男 is formed by two parts. The top part 田 means 'rice paddy', and the bottom part 力 means 'strength'. So the character 男 is related to the idea of a male laboring in a rice paddy.

The seven strokes are drawn in this order:

 nán
(7 strokes)

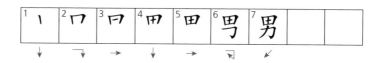

Practice writing this character in the space below,

Can you guess what character you can combine this with to get the word for 'man'? Write the word for 'man' in Chinese characters here:

_____   _____   _____

COMPLETING UNIT 4

Check your understanding

🔊 **04.08** Listen to this audio rehearsal, which asks questions in Mandarin, followed by a short answer.

Combine the answer with the verb in the question to give the full answer.

Feel free to pause or replay the audio as often as you need.

Example: Nǐ yǒu dìdi ma? Méiyǒu. → Méiyǒu, wǒ méiyǒu dìdi.

Show what you know...

Here's what you've just learned. Write or say an example for each item in the list.
Then check off the ones you know.

☐ Give the Chinese phrases for 'my mom', 'my dad', 'your sister', 'your brother' and another family member of your choice.
☐ Give two phrases you can use to express how you 'spend time' or what you 'plan' to do.
☐ Talk about something you would like to do that you haven't yet done.

COMPLETE YOUR MISSION

It's time to complete your mission: describe someone close to you. To do this, you'll need to prepare a description of your friend or family member, share a little bit about where they live or work, their family and all the good things about him or her.

STEP 1: build your script

For you, **shéi shì zuì zhòngyào de rén?** (Who is the most important person?) Use the phrases you've learned and 'me-specific' vocab to build scripts about your favorite person.

Be sure to:

⋯➤ say who it is (**wǒ de péngyou, wǒ de mèimei, wǒ de āyí**)
⋯➤ explain why the person is so important to you

→ describe things you do together (**yìqǐ**)

→ say how long you've known each other (ex. **wǒ rènshi tā liǎng nián le**)

→ describe their characteristics, hobbies, family, etc.

Write down your script, then repeat it until you feel confident.

_____

_____

_____

_____

Use your language to communicate with real people! You need to speak and use a language for it to start to take hold in your long-term memory. And it's the best way to see and feel your progress.

STEP 2: keep it real ... online

This is a script you'll use over and over to talk about your nearest and dearest in Chinese. Start using it right away to fill the gaps. Go online, find the mission for Unit 4, and share your recording with the community.

STEP 3: learn from other learners

Remember, your missions help you, but also help others expand their vocab. Your task is to ask a follow-up question in Mandarin to at least three different people, to inspire them to build on their scripts just a little bit more.

STEP 4: reflect on what you learned

What new words or phrases did you realize you need to start filling gaps?

_____

_____

_____

HEY, LANGUAGE HACKER, YOU'RE DOING GREAT!

You've successfully overcome one of the biggest challenges in language learning: getting started and then keeping it up. Momentum will take you a long way in learning Mandarin quickly, so you should feel good about how far you've come. Always focus on what you can do today that you couldn't do yesterday. Next up: you'll apply what you know to prepare for conversations at the Mandarin dinner table.

Jiāyóu!

5 DESCRIBING YOUR FUTURE PLANS

Mission

Imagine this – you want to spend a few weeks exploring Asia, but you can only afford the trip if your Chinese-speaking friend comes with you and splits the cost.

Your mission is to make an offer they can't refuse! Describe the trip of your dreams and convince a friend to take the trip with you. Use **kěyǐ** to draw the person in and say all the wonderful things you'll do together. Be prepared to explain how you'll get there and how you'll spend your time.

This mission will help you expand your conversation skills by talking about your future plans and using new sequencing phrases for better Mandarin flow.

Mission prep:

⋯⋗ Develop a conversation strategy for breaking the ice: **kěyǐ ma?**
⋯⋗ Talk about your future travel plans with **wǒ yào ...**
⋯⋗ Describe your plans in a sequence: **qián, xiànzài, ránhòu ...**
⋯⋗ Learn essential travel vocab.
⋯⋗ Explore Chinese word order in-depth.
⋯⋗ Memorize a script that you're likely to say often.

BUILDING LANGUAGE FOR STRIKING UP A CONVERSATION

It takes a bit of courage to get started practicing your Mandarin. But preparing 'ice breakers' in advance helps a lot! In this unit, you'll build a ready-made script you can use to start any conversation. You'll learn how to make conversations with Mandarin speakers more casual, and hopefully even make a new friend or two!

#LANGUAGEHACK:
say exponentially more by memorizing regularly-used scripts

CONVERSATION 1

Excuse me, do you speak Mandarin?

CULTURE TIP: *Chinese across the world*
Chinese is one of the most widely spoken native languages in Asia and an official language in **Zhōngguó** (China), **Táiwān** (Taiwan), and **Xīnjiāpō** (Singapore). You'll also find Chinese-speaking minorities all over the world!

Lucy is back at her local language group. Today she wants to build up her confidence to approach someone new and strike up a conversation.

🔊 **05.01** What phrases does Lucy use to approach someone new?

Kěyǐ can also be used by itself to mean 'could do'. Answering a request with **Kěyǐ!** is very common.

> **Lucy :** Qǐngwèn, nín huì shuō Zhōngwén ma?
>
> **Wǎntíng :** Huì. Wǒ shì **Táiwān** rén.
>
> **Lucy :** Tài hǎo le. Wǒ gēn nín shuō Zhōngwén, **kěyǐ** ma?
>
> **Wǎntíng :** Kěyǐ, kěyǐ. Méi wèntí.
>
> **Lucy :** Wǒ jiào Lucy. Nín jiào shénme míngzi?
>
> **Wǎntíng :** Wǒ jiào Wǎntíng. Nǐ xué Zhōngwén xué le duōjiǔ le?
>
> **Lucy :** Wǒ shì gānggāng kāishǐ de.
>
> **Wǎntíng :** Nǐ shì gānggāng kāishǐ de ma? Dànshì nǐ shuō Zhōngwén shuō de hěn hǎo.
>
> **Lucy:** Zhēnde ma?
>
> **Wǎntíng :** Zhēnde! Nǐ shuō de hěn hǎo! Wǒmen kāishǐ ba!

FIGURE IT OUT

1 Use context and familiar words to answer the questions in Chinese:

a What question does Lucy ask to approach Wăntíng?

_____

_____

b Where does Wăntíng come from?

_____

_____

2 Find and highlight the phrases in the conversation where:

a Wăntíng tells Lucy where she's from.

b Lucy asks to practice Chinese with Wăntíng.

c Wăntíng tells Lucy she speaks Chinese well.

d Wăntíng suggests 'let's start!'.

3 Can you find the phrase Lucy uses to share that she only just started learning Chinese? Use Wăntíng's question about 'how long' as a clue!

Write it here: _____ _____

4 Now find these three words in the conversation and highlight them.

a The second part of the structure used to say 'with', which means 'together' when it is used alone. What is this word? _____

b The word 'can' is used as 'can/could' three times in the dialogue. Find the word and write it here: _____

c Wăntíng exclaims, 'Really!' What is this word in Chinese? _____

5 Want to learn several useful replies in Chinese? Here are three useful expressions you'll find in the dialogue in addition to **kěyǐ** (could do; lit. 'can'). Write out the following phrases:

a That's great. _____ _____

b No problem (lit. 'no question') _____

_____

c Really? _____ _____

NOTICE

🔊 05.02 Listen to the audio and study the table.

Essential phrases for Conversation 1

Chinese	Meaning	Literal translation
Táiwān rén	from Taiwan	Taiwan person
Tài hǎo le	That's great	Extremely good [change marker]
kěyǐ	can, could	can, could
gānggāng	just	just
kāishǐ	to start	start
shì ... de	[emphasizes something that happened in the past]	is ... of
shuō de hěn hǎo	speak well	speak of very good
Wǒmen kāishǐ ba!	Let's start!	We start [suggestion marker]!

CONVERSATION STRATEGY: introducing yourself

If you meet a stranger and see an opportunity to practice, there's a more polite form of the word for 'you' in Chinese – it's **nín**. In certain situations, it's safer to introduce yourself using the formal (polite) form, **nín**, at first. And if you know the person's name, you can use their surname and title (e.g. Wáng Lǎoshī).

If you don't know the other person's name and it's not in a work situation, you can also use:

āyí	aunt, for a woman a generation older than you
shūshu	uncle, for a man a generation older than you
gēge	brother, for a man slightly older than you
dìdi	brother, for a man slightly younger than you
jiějie	sister, for a woman slightly older than you
mèimei	sister, for a woman slightly younger than you

1 Write out these two phrases from the dialogue you can use when approaching someone to practice Chinese.

a Excuse me, do you speak Chinese?

_____

_____

b I want to speak Chinese with you, could/can I?

_____

_____

2 Match the phrases with the correct forms.

a **Nín hǎo.**   **1** Could we? (lit. can?)

b **Kěyǐ ma?**   **2** How have you been lately, Teacher Wang?

c **Wáng Lǎoshī zuìjìn zěnmeyàng?**   **3** Hello. (formal)

d **Nǐ hǎo.**   **4** Hello. (informal)

CULTURE TIP: _using nín_
Until now, you've seen **nǐ** used as the word for 'you'. You'll use **nǐ** when chatting to people you know well; young people use it amongst themselves, even with people they don't know that well. But in the conversation, you'll notice Lucy starts by using **nín** instead – the 'formal you' in Chinese – since she doesn't know Wǎntíng yet. Wǎntíng shifts the conversation to a more casual tone when she introduces herself using her first name.

GRAMMAR EXPLANATION: adverbs

In the dialogue, you may have noticed the structure **shuō de**. Here are a few other ways you might see or hear it:

shuō de bù hǎo	**shuō de hěn hǎo**	**shuō de hěn qīngchu**
to not speak well	to speak very well	to speak very clearly

The verb + **de** structure is a common way to attach adverbs to a verb. Here's a few more examples:

chī de hěn kuài	**chī de hěn màn**
to eat very fast	to eat very slow

Example: Tāmen wán de hěn kāixīn. (They have a lot of fun.)

Now, it's your turn.

1 How would you say 'to speak very fast'?

2 How would you say to 'to eat very well'?

3 What about 'to not speak slowly'?

When I was learning Chinese in Taiwan, I kept asking myself 'Why do they have to say it like that?' But with the benefit of hindsight, I've grown to love how Chinese works! It's actually more flexible than English in many ways, but it does take a bit of practice to get used to the different ways it works. So while we're getting used to it, let's have some fun with it!

PRACTICE

Here's the big question: Why do you see **wǒ xiǎng** in some instances in Chinese, but **wǒ yào** in others?

In both Chinese and English, sentences like 'I want (to)' and 'I will' both indicate a possible action in the future or a request. And as in English, they each have slightly different meanings and uses. Let's take a look.

Example.

Yào:

⋯⋗ When followed by a noun like kāfēi (coffee), chá (tea) or shuǐ (water), means 'I want' and it implies a certain degree of immediacy.

⋯⋗ When followed by a verb, it means 'want to'.

⋯⋗ Can be used to indicate something you plan to do in the future. For example, xīngqīèr wǒ yào qù Shànghǎi (I will go / want to go to Shanghai on Tuesday).

Xiǎng:

⋯⋗ When followed by a noun, means 'to miss'. So wǒ xiǎng kāfēi doesn't mean 'I would like coffee' but 'I miss coffee'.

⋯⋗ When followed by a verb means 'would like to'.

1 Circle the appropriate verb in each of the examples below:

 a Wǒmen dōu xiǎng / yào guǒzhī. (We all want juice.)

 b Nǐ xiǎng / yào hóngsè de háishì báisè de? (Do you want the red one or the white one?)

 c Wǒ xiǎng / yào nǐ. (I miss you.)

2 Use the appropriate verb to translate the following sentences:

 a I would like to go to Xi'an.

 _____

 _____

 b I want water.

 _____

 _____

c I want to study.

_____

_____

d I miss my mom.

_____

_____

e I will go to Guilin.

_____

_____

GRAMMAR EXPLANATION: word order

'Named must your fear be, before banish it you can!' – Yoda

Chinese word order is a little similar to English word order, especially at the basic level. In simple sentences, the structure is SVO (subject–verb–object), just like in English. For example, 'I eat bread' is **wǒ chī miànbāo**. As you start building longer sentences, there are a few differences you'll likely notice.

Adding time to a sentence

Time words like **xiànzài** or **jīntiān** go at the beginning of the sentence, either before or after the subject.

Example: 'I work today' could be **wǒ jīntiān gōngzuò** or **jīntiān wǒ gōngzuò**.

Adding location to a sentence

Location words – where the action in the sentence takes place – goes between the time word or subject if there is no time word and the verb phrase.

Example: 'I work at home today' would be **wǒ jīntiān zài jiāli gōngzuò**.

Adding duration to a sentence

Duration has a different set of rules than other time words and it typically goes after the verb phrase.

Example: 'Next month I'm working in Beijing for one week' would be **wǒ xiàge yuè zài Běijīng gōngzuò yí ge xīngqī**.

1 Mix and match phrases you've learned with new vocab. Use the phrases given in the box to create six new sentences in Chinese.

> **Wǒmen shì** (we are), **wǒmen gōngzuò** (we work/we are working), **wǒmen qù** (we go/we're going), **wǒmen chī** (we eat/we're eating), **zài fànguǎn** (at the restaurant), **zài shātān** (at the beach), **měi shí měi kè** (all the time), **yí ge rén** (alone), **zài lǚtú zhōng** (on a trip)

a _____ _____

b _____ _____

c _____ _____

d _____ _____

e _____ _____

f _____ _____

2 Put the following words in the correct order to form sentences:

a **wǒ** / **zài Běijīng** / **jīnnián** / **liù ge yuè** / **xué le** – (This year I studied in Beijing for six months.)

_____

_____

b **nǐ** / **chī** / **xīngqīwǔ** / **zài fànguǎn** – (You eat at the restaurant Friday.)

_____

_____

c **měinián** / **wǒmen** / **gōngzuò** / **zài Xiānggǎng** / **yícì** – (We work in Hong Kong once every year.)

_____

_____

#LANGUAGEHACK: say exponentially more by memorizing regularly-used scripts

A lot of people get nervous speaking to someone new for the first time – especially in another language. But when you plan out what you'll say in advance, you have less to worry about. Luckily, many conversations follow a similar pattern, and you can use this to your advantage.

Learn set phrases

Sometimes you may want to say a complicated phrase that you haven't learned the structure of yet. But just because you don't know the grammar behind a phrase doesn't mean you can't use it. In these cases, you can simply memorize the full phrase as a chunk so you can use it whenever you need to – even if you don't fully understand all the individual words.

Try this with the very useful power phrase **... kěyǐ ma?**, which can be used in a variety of situations and conversation topics.

Memorize a script

When you learn set phrases that are specific to you and combine them together, you create a personal 'script' you can use over and over again.

For instance, over the course of my travels I'm frequently asked, 'Why are you learning this language?' and I'm often asked about my work as a writer, which isn't easy to explain as a beginner. Because I know these questions are coming, I don't need to answer spontaneously every time. Instead, I craft a solid response in advance so I can speak confidently when the question inevitably comes up.

For you, it may be your upcoming travels to China, or the personal reasons you're learning the language. Ultimately, if you know you'll need to give an explanation or mini story

You can ride a bike without understanding aerodynamics, you can use a computer even if you don't know the physics of how circuits work ... and you can use Chinese phrases at the right time, even if you don't understand each word and why they go together the way they do!

GRAMMAR TIP:
kěyǐ ma?
If you use **kěyǐ ma?** (could I/we?) in a sentence like this, this chunk will go to the end of the sentence.

You can even have a native speaker review your scripts and refine them to good Chinese. It's fine to speak spontaneously with mistakes, but you may as well get it right if you're memorizing it in advance. It's easy and free when you know where to look. See our Resources to find out how to get free help online.

frequently, memorize it to have ready when it's time to produce.

First decide what you want to say. Make it personal to you. Then simplify it as much as possible to remove complicated expressions.

If possible, try to do this in Chinese from the start. Think of key words and phrases and jot them down. Then you can fill in the script later. If you find this tricky, think of it in English and then try to translate that.

Finally, when you have your final script, recite it as often as you can until you commit it to memory.

PUT IT TOGETHER

1 Imagine that you're planning to visit China. In what situations might you need to ask the question, **kěyǐ ma**? Use this phrase along with your dictionary to create sentences you could use:

⋯⟫ at a social event (e.g. '... I speak with you?')
⋯⟫ at a café (e.g. '... I sit here?')
⋯⟫ in the park (e.g. '... I ride my bike?')
⋯⟫ at someone's house (e.g. '... I use the bathroom?').

2 Pick one of the following situations, then prepare a short script you can use without having to think on the spot.

⋯⟫ **Situation 1:** Memorize a few words you can say any time someone unexpected hits you with Chinese. Suggestions: 'Ah, you speak Chinese!' 'I just started.' 'I've been learning Chinese for ...'

···➔ **Situation 2:** Someone asks you to give a mini life story or asks why you are learning Chinese. Suggestion: 'I like the language!' ←

···➔ **Situation 3:** You need to interrupt someone on the street to ask a question in Chinese. Suggestions: 'Excuse me.' 'May I ask?'

This is a great memorized script to have in your back pocket. You'll use it a lot. You may know a few phrases that you can use to discuss this, but it's good to have a go - to answer for this question memorized.

CONVERSATION 2

Where are you going?

Since Lucy and Wǎntíng are both visitors to Beijing, travel is a natural conversation topic. In fact, as you learn any new language, you'll likely be asked (or want to ask someone) about traveling to different places.

◀)) 05.03 What phrase does Wǎntíng use to ask, 'Do you travel a lot?'

> **Wǎntíng:** Nǐ shi shénme shíhou lái dào Běijīng de? Nǐ chángcháng lǚxíng ma?
>
> **Lucy :** Bù cháng. Wǒ shì sān ge yuè qián lái dào Běijīng de. Ránhòu, wǒ yào **chūqù** Rìběn.
>
> **Wǎntíng :** Nǐ de yìsi shì nǐ yào 'qù' Rìběn?
>
> **Lucy :** Duì. Shì de. Xièxie. Wǒ yào qù Rìběn.
>
> **Wǎntíng :** Nǐ yīnggāi qù Táiwān. Táiwān yǒu hěn duō piàoliang de dìfang.
>
> **Lucy :** Wǒ kěnéng xiàtiān zài qù. Běijīng hái yǒu hěn duō wǒ méi qù guo de dìfang. Wǒ xiǎng duō lǚxíng. Wǒ hái xiǎng qù Zhōngguó de qítā chéngshì kànkan.
>
> **Wǎntíng :** Lìrú …
>
> **Lucy :** Xī'ān, Guìlín, Sūzhōu … Wǒ xiǎng cóng Rìběn huílái yǐhòu jiù qù.
>
> **Wǎntíng :** Nǐ shuō de **duì**. Dànshì zài Běijīng hái yǒu hěn duō hǎowán de dìfang nǐ kěyǐ qù!

GRAMMAR TIP:
qù versus *chūqù*
Both **qù** and **chūqù** can mean 'to go', but **chūqù** includes a complement to indicate the direction of the verb, which in this case is 'to go out'. Common complements that can be paired with **qù** (to go) or **lái** (to come) are **xià** (down), **shàng** (up), **chū** (out), **jìn** (in) and **huí** (back). Together you can construct complements like **xiàlái** (come down), **chūlái** (come out) and **jìnqù** (go in).

VOCABULARY: *duì*
Duì is a great chunk meaning 'that's right'. You'll often hear this with an 'a' as **duì a** to change the tone to be a bit softer.

CONVERSATION 2 ···➔ **97**

FIGURE IT OUT

1 Find and highlight the following phrases:

a What is the phrase Wǎntíng uses to ask, 'How long have you been in Beijing?'

_____

_____

b Lucy answers that she has been in Beijing for three months. What is 'for three months' in Chinese? Hint: it's literally 'three months before' in this context.

_____

_____

c After Wǎntíng corrects Lucy, Lucy says: 'Right. That's it.' What is 'that's it' in Chinese?

_____

_____

2 What phrase does Wǎntíng use to correct Lucy when she makes a mistake?

_____

_____

3 Use context along with words you know to figure out:

a where Lucy wants to go after China _____

b where Wǎntíng suggests that Lucy visit. _____

4 Look over the dialogue to figure out which words you should use to fill in the gaps:

a **Yǒu hěn duō** _____ **de dìfang.** (There are many pretty places.)

b _____ **xiàtiān.** (Maybe in the summer.)

c **Wǒ xiǎng** _____ **lǚxíng.** (I would like to travel more.)

d **Wǒ xiǎng qù Zhōngguó de** _____ **chéngshì.** (I would like to visit other cities.)

5 What is the word Lucy uses to say 'for example' when asking Wǎntíng for a list of cities she'd like to go to? _____

NOTICE

🔊 **05.04** Listen to the audio and study the table.

Essential phrases for Conversation 2

Chinese	Meaning	Literal translation
lái dào	came	come arrive
chángcháng lǚxíng	travel often	often travel
bù cháng	not often	not often
ránhòu	then	then
qián	before	before
nǐ de yìsi shì ...	you mean ...	you of meaning is ...
duì	correct	correct
shì de	that's it	is of
yīnggāi	should	should
hěn duō	very many	very many
piàoliang de dìfang	pretty places	pretty of place
xiàtiān	summer	summer
lǚxíng	to travel	to travel
qítā chéngshì	other cities	other city
lìrú ...	for example ...	for example ...
děng	to wait	to wait

1 How would you correct yourself in Chinese by saying 'I mean ...'?

2 How would you ask in Chinese, 'Do you mean ...?'

3 Notice how the word 'thing' has different translations in Chinese depending on if it's a person, place, object (**dōngxi**) or idea or matter (**shìqing**). How would you complete the following?

   a **Wǒ xǐhuan chī hěnduō** _____ (I like to eat a lot of things.)

   b **Wǒ yǒu hěnduō** _____ **xūyào xué**. (I have a lot of things to study.)

   c **Wǒ yīnggāi mǎi duōshao** _____? (How many things should I buy?)

4 Match the Mandarin phrases with the correct English translations.

a	nǐ chángcháng lǚxíng	1	you should go to ...
b	nǐ de yìsi shì	2	you can do ...
c	nǐ yīnggāi qù ...	3	you travel often
d	hái yǒu hěnduō	4	you mean
e	děng	5	still so much
f	nǐ kěyǐ ...	6	wait

5 Highlight the correct translation for each word or phrase:

a	kěnéng	maybe/since
b	qián	before/after
c	qítā	other/one
d	hěn duō	more/so much
e	gèng duō	other/even more

VOCABULARY: zǒu
(to go/to walk)
Zǒu is typically
translated as 'to go'
and tends to be used to
say 'let's go' – **Wǒmen
zǒu ba**. On its own,
it can also mean 'to
walk'. For other modes
of transport, different
verbs are used including
qí when going by bike,
kāi when going by car
and **zuò** when going by
train or plane.

CULTURE TIP: *riding
the China Railway
High-speed (CRH)*
While in China, you'll
have the option to
take the **Zhōngguó
gāosù tiělù** (China
Railway High-speed or
CRH). The trains come
regularly, and they
cover 33 of China's 34
provinces.

Here's some additional vocab you can use to talk about your own travel plans.

Zuò huǒchē/fēijī	go by train/plane
Qí zìxíngchē	go by bike
Zǒu	go by foot
Kāichē	go by car

PRONUNCIATION EXPLANATION: tone changes

Previously, you learned that the tone for **bù** changes to second tone (**bú**) when the word that follows is fourth tone, like **qù**. In addition to this change, there are two other tone changes that you need to learn to properly pronounce Mandarin.

Tone changes for yī

When followed by a fourth tone, **yī** becomes **yí** (second tone). And when followed by any other tone, **yī** changes to **yì** (fourth tone). It's only when **yī** appears in a series, a larger number, an address or a date that **yī** remains first tone, regardless of the next tone.

These three tone
- change rules are
the main tone
changes you need to
memorize because
they tend to appear
often. There isn't
a huge number of
verbs that work like
this, but the ones
that do tend to be
used a lot. You will
soon get a feel for
what sounds right!

🔊 **05.05** Here are a few examples:

yí ge	one [measure word]
yìqǐ	together
yī èr sān	one two three

Tone changes for third tone

When two third tones appear side by side, as in **nǐ hǎo**, the first of the two is pronounced as second tone. So even though you'll see **nǐ hǎo** written with two third tones, it's pronounced as **ní hǎo**.

🔊 **05.06** Here are a few examples:

hén hǎo

kéyǐ

ní hǎo

1 These common words and expressions each require a tone change. Practice pronouncing them with the proper changes.

    a suǒyǐ (so, therefore)

    b shuǐguǒ (fruit)

    c hěn yuǎn (very far)

2 Now practice marking the tones in regards to pronunciation with the rules you've just learned.

    a yī bàn   ⟶ _____

    b bù shì   ⟶ _____

    c yīyàng (the same) ⟶ _____

    d yǔfǎ (grammar) ⟶ _____

PUT IT TOGETHER

Read the questions as well as the prompts in Chinese. Then reply in sentences relevant to your life. Use your dictionary to look up the 'me-specific' vocab you need.

a Do you travel a lot? (... **yìdiǎn** ... **bù cháng**)

Wǒ _____ _____

b Where are you going for your next trip?

Wǒ qù _____ _____

c How long are you going for? (... **yí ge yuè** ... **yì tiān**)

Wǒ _____ _____

d When are you going? (... **bā yuè** ... **xià ge xīngqī**)

Wǒ _____ _____

e How are you going to travel? (... **zuò fēijī** ... **zǒulù**)

Wǒ _____ _____

MORE CHINESE CHARACTERS

In this unit, you'll learn the Chinese characters for several commonly used Chinese words.

个 gè

The character for the measure word **gè** is 个. Because it is a measure for 人 (person or people), it has the radical 人 at its top. It's a simple character with three strokes. They are drawn in the following order:

个 **gè**
(3 strokes)

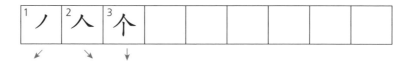

Practice writing this character in the space below.

好 hǎo

The Chinese character for 'good' may look partly familiar because the left component in the character is the character for 'female'. The right component is 子, the component for 'child'.

'Good' has six strokes. They are written in this order:

女子 hǎo (hào)
(6 strokes)

Practice writing this character in the space below.

去 qù

The character 去 meaning 'to go' refers to 'going to a place'. The top half of the character includes 土, pronounced **tǔ**, meaning 'earth'.

The character for 'to go' is written with five strokes. They are written in this order:

去 qù
(5 strokes)

Practice writing this character in the space below.

来 lái

The last character you'll learn in this unit is the character for 'to come' in Chinese. 木 is in this character. It means 'wood' or 'tree'. You can imagine 来 representing birds which 'come' to a tree.

The character for 'to come' is written in seven strokes. They are drawn in this order:

来 lái
(7 strokes)

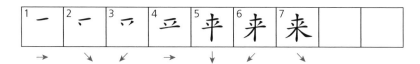

Practice writing this character in the space below.

COMPLETING UNIT 5

Check your understanding

You know the drill! Listen to the audio rehearsal, which will ask you questions in Chinese. Use what you've learned to answer the questions in Chinese with details about yourself.

🔊 05.07 To check that you understand the audio, don't forget that you can always look at the transcript online!

⋯⟩ **Nǐ shénme shíhou qù Shànghǎi?**

⋯⟩ **Nǐ zěnme qù?**

⋯⟩ **Nǐ chángcháng lǚxíng ma?**

Show what you know ...

Here's what you've just learned. Write or say an example for each item in the list.
Then check off the ones you know.

- ☐ Give three ways for politely addressing someone you don't know well.
- ☐ Ask a polite question using 'Could we ...'?
- ☐ Use **wǒ yào** to say something you will do tomorrow, this weekend or next year.
- ☐ Give two sentences, one using 'should' and one using 'need'.
- ☐ Give three modes of transport in Chinese.
- ☐ Give the Chinese words to say 'now', 'later' and 'before'.

COMPLETE YOUR MISSION

It's time to complete your mission: convince your friend to go with you on your adventure. To do this, you'll need to describe the trip of your dreams.

CULTURE TIP: *know before you go!*
This is a good time to expand on your script with some of your own research!
There are many beautiful cities in China, Taiwan and Singapore. Look into
what sights there are and what you can do when you get there. If you can, talk
to someone who lives there to get the inside scoop. Your language partners
can be a great resource for tips and stories on travel and culture! Plus, travel
aspirations are a great conversation starter.

Travel is a popular
topic among language
learners, so this is a
script you'll want to
make sure you have
down solid.

STEP 1: build your script

Create a script you can use to tell other language hackers about your
travel plans. Incorporate as many new words or phrases from this unit as
possible. Be sure to say:

- ⋯⋗ where you're going and what you plan to do when you get there
- ⋯⋗ what you want to see first (what are you most excited to explore?)
- ⋯⋗ when you'd like to go and how long you'd like to be there
- ⋯⋗ how you'll get there and how you'll get around once you're there.

Give recommendations to other language hackers for things to do at this
destination! Write down your script, then repeat it until you feel confident.

Give and get feedback from other learners – it will massively improve your Mandarin! When the opportunity presents itself in real life, you won't always have notes at the ready, so let's emulate this by having you speak your script from memory.

STEP 2: feedback promotes learning ... online

This time, when you make your recording, you're not allowed to read your script! Instead, speak your phrases to the camera, relying on brief notes, or even better, say your script from memory. Make sure to study it well!

STEP 3: learn from other learners

How do other language hackers describe their travel plans and dreams? Your task is to listen and choose a vacation you'd like to join in on. Say why you think the place and plans sound good.

STEP 4: reflect on what you learned

What would you like to add to your script next?

HEY, LANGUAGE HACKER, YOU'RE HALFWAY THERE!

Isn't it easier when you already know what you want to say? If you take advantage of how predictable some conversations can be and prepare answers you'll give often, you can be confident in what you say. Next, let's build on your script to talk about your friends and family.

Nǐ néng zuò dào! (You can do it!)

6 HAVE SOME FOOD, DRINK AND CONVERSATION

Mission

Imagine this – you've discovered an incredible restaurant near your house, so you invite a new Chinese friend to join you there. You can't wait to show off your insider knowledge. But it turns out, to your horror, that your friend has heard bad things about it! **Nà**, he says, **bú tài hǎo …**

Your mission is to convince your friend to come with you to the restaurant. Be prepared to give your opinion and say why you disagree. Back it up with details of why the place is so **shòu huānyíng** (popular) – describe food you like and why you like it.

This mission will help you get comfortable agreeing or disagreeing and explaining your point of view, as well as talking about food and restaurants – a very important topic.

Mission prep:

⋯⟩ Learn how to order food.
⋯⟩ Develop the ability to talk about what you like to eat and drink.
⋯⟩ Learn how to talk about what you want to do.
⋯⟩ Know how to discuss future plans.
⋯⟩ Learn how to make comparisons.
⋯⟩ Identify and write four important Chinese radicals and the characters you'll see them in.

BUILDING LANGUAGE FOR CHINESE DINNER CONVERSATIONS

Having a long meal filled with fun discussion is a key part of Chinese culture. To blend in, it's important for you to be able to proudly share your opinions. A lot of your conversations will take place in cafés or restaurants, so let's make sure you also understand the different ways you'll interact with servers, as well as with your dinner companion.

#LANGUAGEHACK:
sound more fluent with conversation connectors

CONVERSATION 1

I'll have ...

VOCABULARY TIP:
zhè'er
Depending on where you visit, you'll hear different words for 'here' in Chinese. **Zhè'er** is what you'll most likely hear in Beijing. **Zhèli** is what you'll hear further south and in Taiwan.

Ordering in Chinese restaurants may be different from what you're used to. When interacting with servers, you'll need to signal for their attention rather than them coming to check on you regularly.

🔊 **06.01** Lucy and her friend Xiǎowēi are sitting down to eat at a café in Beijing. What phrase does the **fúwùyuán** (waiter) use to ask, 'Are you ready?'

CULTURE TIP:
zhájiàngmiàn
Zhájiàngmiàn is a typical Chinese food particularly popular in Beijing. It's made from wheat noodles with a **zhájiàng** sauce – a sauce made from ground beef or pork and fermented soybean. It's topped with fresh or pickled vegetables like edamame, carrots or cucumber.

Notice that while in English we'd say 'I'll have' or 'I'd like', the Chinese say **wǒ yào**, (I want).

CULTURE TIP: rè shuǐ
When you order **rè shuǐ**, or even **shuǐ**, you'll probably get hot or warm water, which is the default choice in most parts of China.

Lucy :	Wǒ dùzi è le! A, fúwùyuán lái le.
Fúwùyuán :	Huānyíng guānglín. Nǐmen shì liǎng wèi ma?
Xiǎowēi :	Duì. Wǒmen shì liǎng ge rén.
Fúwùyuán :	Qǐng gēn wǒ lái. Nǐmen kěyǐ zuò zài **zhè'er**. Zhè shì càidān.
Xiǎowēi :	Wǒmen yào hē rè chá.
Fúwùyuán :	Méi wèntí. Wǒ mǎshàng huílái.
Fúwùyuán :	Zhǔnbèi hǎo le ma?
Xiǎowēi :	Zhǔnbèi hǎo le.
Fúwùyuán :	Nǐmen yào diǎn shénme?
Lucy :	Wǒmen yào yì wǎn **zhájiàngmiàn**, yì pán xīhóngshì chǎo jīdàn …
Xiǎowēi :	Hái yào yì wǎn suānlà tāng …
Lucy :	Suānlà tāng hěn là ma?
Xiǎowēi :	Bú là. Hěn hǎochī. Nǐ yīnggāi cháng yi cháng.
Fúwùyuán :	Hái yào bié de ma?
Xiǎowēi :	Jiù zhèyàng.
Lucy :	Qíshí, **wǒ yào** yì bēi **rè shuǐ**.
Fúwùyuán :	Hǎo de. Suǒyǐ, yì wǎn zhájiàngmiàn, yì pán xīhóngshì chǎo jīdàn, yì wǎn suānlà tāng, hé yì bēi rè shuǐ …
Xiǎowēi :	Duì.

FIGURE IT OUT

1 Use what you find in the conversation to write out in Chinese:

   a two people (formal) _____

   b two people (informal) _____

   c I'm hungry! _____

   d This is the menu. _____

2 When the waiter returns to the table, he asks Xiǎowēi and Lucy two
   questions. In the first, he asks if they are ready. What do you think the
   second question means?

   _____

   _____

3 Highlight the dishes Xiǎowēi and Lucy order and write them below.
   Hint: they each start with the Chinese word for 'one':

   a _____   _____

   b _____   _____

   c _____   _____

   d _____   _____

4 Each of these translations from the conversation is **cuò**. Determine
   what word makes each one **cuò** and correct it.

   a **Wǒ yǐjing huílái.** ⟶ I'll be right back _____   _____

   b **Hěn tián ma?** ⟶ Is it spicy? _____   _____

CULTURE TIP: *ge rèn*

While you can expect to hear this kind of formal language in restaurants or other similar settings, you can use **ge rén** when talking about yourself, groups of people that include yourself or in less formal situations.

NOTICE

🔊 **06.02** Listen to the audio and study the table.

Essential phrases for Conversation 1

Chinese	Meaning	Literal translation
Wǒ dúzi è le!	I'm hungry!	I stomach hungry [change marker]!
fúwùyuán	waiter	waiter
Huānyíng guānglín.	Welcome.	Welcome.
liǎng wèi	two people (formal)	two people
Qǐng gēn wǒ lái.	Please come with me.	Please with me come.
zuò	to sit	sit
zhè'er	here	here
càidān	menu	menu
hē rè chá	drink hot tea	drink hot tea
Wǒ mǎshàng huílái.	I'll be right back.	I immediately return come.
Zhǔnbèi hǎo le.	Ready.	Prepare good [change marker].
diǎn	to order	order
zhájiàngmiàn	noodles with soybean paste	noodles with soybean paste
yì wǎn	one bowl	one [measure word for bowl]
yì pán	one plate	one [measure word for plate]
xīhóngshì chǎo jīdàn	stir-fried tomatoes and scrambled egg	stir-fried tomatoes and scrambled egg
suānlà tāng	hot and sour soup	hot and sour soup
là	spicy	spicy
Hái yào bié de ma?	Anything else?	Still want other of [question marker]?
Jiù zhèyàng.	That's all.	Just this way.
qíshí	actually	actually
yì bēi	one cup	one [measure word for cup]
shuǐ	water	water
Hěn hǎo chī.	It's tasty.	Very good eat.

1 Look at 'I'm hungry' in the phrase list. How does Chinese express this feeling differently than you would in English?

_____

_____

2 Write out three measure words in the conversation that are used to order one of an item.

a one bowl _____ **b** one plate _____ **c** one cup _____

3 Find and write out the following adjectives (describing words like 'cold') from the conversation:

a hot _____ **b** ready _____ **c** spicy _____

4 What do the phrases and questions mean? Match them to the English answers.

a Huānyíng guānglín.

b Qǐng gēn wǒ lái.

c Méi wèntí.

d Wǒ mǎshàng huílái.

e Zhǔnbèi hǎo le ma?

f Nǐmen yào diǎn shénme?

g Nǐ yīnggāi cháng yi cháng.

h Hái yào bié de ma?

i Jiù zhèyàng.

j Qíshí ...

1 I'll be right back.

2 Are you ready?

3 Come with me please.

4 Do you want anything else?

5 Actually ...

6 Welcome.

7 You should try.

8 That's all.

9 No problem.

10 What do you want to order?

PRACTICE

1 Fill in the gaps with the missing words in Chinese.

a Nǐ yào _____ shénme? (Do you want to order?)

b Wǒ yào yì _____ rè chá. (I want a cup of hot tea.)

c Wǒ _____ yì wǎn suānlà tāng. (I want a bowl of hot and sour soup.)

d Wǒ bù xǐhuan _____ (I don't like spicy.)

e Wǒ bù néng _____ là de. (I can't eat spicy.)

f Nǐ dùzi _____ le ma? (Are you hungry?)

Here's some more important vocab related to eating and drinking to give you a solid base. Before you head to a Chinese restaurant, it's a good idea to learn the names of your favorite dishes in advance.

EATING AND DRINKING VOCABULARY

🔊 06.03 Listen to the audio for the following table.

Chinese	Meaning	Literal translation	Chinese	Meaning	Literal translation
Wǒ dùzi è le	I am hungry	I stomach hungry [change marker]	cān	food/meal	meal
Wǒ kǒu kě le	I am thirsty	I throat thirsty [change marker]	hǎo chī	delicious	good eat
chī	to eat	eat	zǎocān	breakfast	early meal
hē	to drink	drink	wǔcān	lunch	afternoon meal
zuòfàn	to cook	make rice	wǎncān	dinner	late meal
sù	vegetarian	vegetarian	ròu	meat	meat
jiā	with	add	jī ròu	chicken	chicken meat
Nǐ yǒu shénme tuījiàn de ma?	What do you recommend?	You have what recommendation of [question marker]?	niú ròu	beef	cow meat
Wǒ duì huāshēng guòmǐn	I'm allergic to peanuts.	I against peanuts allergic.	zhū ròu	pork	pig meat
Wǒ yào jiā ...	I want with	I want add	yú	fish	fish
			hǎixiān	seafood	seafood
			shūcài	vegetables	vegetables
			shuǐguǒ	fruit	fruit

2 What are your favorite foods? What can you imagine yourself asking for in a Chinese restaurant? Add more food or drink items you would order in Chinese. Then add more phrases you could use to interact with the wait staff.

PUT IT TOGETHER

1 Role-play a conversation in which you order your favorite foods in
Chinese at a restaurant. Respond to the question by ordering anything
you like (as long as it's in Chinese!). Take inspiration from what you've
learned in this unit, and use your dictionary to look up new words.

You'll order a starter, a main course, and two drinks. ←————————— *Dùzi è le. and kǒu kě le!* You've already seen the *càidān* and it conveniently has all your favorite foods!

Fúwùyuán : Nín yào diǎn shénme?

    Ni : a _____ _____

Fúwùyuán : Hǎo de. Hái yào bié de ma?

    Ni : b _____ _____

Fúwùyuán : Nín yào hē shénme?

    Ni : c _____ _____

Fúwùyuán : Wǒ mǎshàng huílái. (30 fēnzhōng yǐhòu)

    Ni : d _____ _____ *(call the waiter back)*

Fúwùyuán : Hái yào bié de ma?

    Ni : *(You order another drink.)* e _____ _____

Fúwùyuán : Méi wèntí.

2 Create three 'me-specific' phrases in which you describe your normal
mealtime routine. Use the vocab you've learned in this unit, as well as
any new words you need from your dictionary. Try to include:

What you usually eat (**chī**) or drink (**hē**).

Whether you normally cook (**zuòfàn**), have dinner in a restaurant (**zài
fànguǎn chīfàn**), or microwave yesterday's pizza (**yòng wēibōlú zuò
zuótiān de pīsà**).

CONVERSATION 2

In my opinion …

Lucy and Xiǎowēi discover they don't quite see eye to eye on where they should go in Beijing.

🔊 06.04 How does their disagreement get resolved?

Lucy : Nà, wǒmen xūyào qù Bādálǐng kàn Chángchéng.

Xiǎowēi : Bù, bù. Nàli zǒngshì rénshānrénhǎi! Wǒ jué de zuìhǎo qù Gùgōng.

Lucy : Wǒ zhīdào, wǒmen yīnggāi dōu qù. Dànshì Chángchéng bìkàn.

Xiǎowēi : Wǒ bù tóngyì. Zài wǒ kànlái, Gùgōng gèng yǒu yìsi. Guàng wán Gùgōng yǐhòu, wǒmen yǐjing zài hútòng fùjìn …

Lucy : Duì, Gùgōng méiyǒu Chángchéng de rén duō, dànshì Gùgōng méiyǒu Chángchéng de měi jǐng.

Xiǎowēi : Bú duì. Gùgōng hěn yǒu yìsi, hěn měi.

Lucy : Duì. Nǐ shuō de duì … Gùgōng hěn měi, dànshì wǒ jué de yǒudiǎn wúliáo.

Xiǎowēi : Hěn duō Zhōngguó rén hái méi qù guo Gùgōng. Nǐ zhīdao ma?

Lucy : Nà hǎo … Wǒmen kěyǐ tuǒxié. Xiān qù Chángchéng. Wǔcān yǐhòu qù Gùgōng wán. Ránhòu qù hútòng ba.

Xiǎowēi : Hǎo jìhuà – wǒ tóngyì.

FIGURE IT OUT

1 Find the following details within the conversation, then write the answers in English.

   a What are the names of the two tourist sites being discussed?

     Great Wall _____   Forbidden City _____

   b Xiǎowēi doesn't want to go to the Great Wall because it's too crowded. What is the idiomatic expression she uses to say this?

     _____

     _____

   c What is Lucy's opinion of the Forbidden City? She uses two sentences to share her views. Write the phrases in Chinese:

     1 The Forbidden City doesn't have as many people as the Great Wall.

     _____

     _____

     2 The Forbidden City doesn't have the Great Wall's views.

     _____

     _____

   d What phrase shows that Lucy thinks that she and Xiǎowēi should compromise?

     Wǒmen kěyǐ _____

2 Find these phrases in the conversation and highlight them by using the vocabulary you already know as a clue.

   a I don't agree   c a little boring

   b not true   d then

3 Look at the phrases from the conversation and write out the meaning of the words in bold.

   a **Rénshānrénhǎi** _____

   b ... **bìkàn!** _____

   c ... dànshì wǒ jué de **yǒu diǎn** wúliáo. _____

   d Wǒmen kěyǐ **tuǒxié.** _____

NOTICE

🔊 **06.05** Listen to the audio and study the table.

People mountain people sea
In Chinese, to say that it's crowded, you use the expression 'people mountain, people sea'. It expresses that there are so many people they go all the way from the mountains to the sea.

CULTURE TIP: *hútòng*
A **hútòng** is a narrow street where many traditional Chinese houses are located. They are often also filled with restaurants and shops.

Essential phrases for Conversation 2

Chinese	Meaning	Literal translation
Chángchéng	Great Wall	Great Wall
rénshānrénhǎi	crowded	people mountain people sea
gèng hǎo	better	even more good
Gùgōng	Forbidden City	Forbidden City
dōu	all	all
bìkàn	must-see	must-see
tóngyì	agree	agree
Zài wǒkànlái ...	In my opinion ...	Located I see come ...
zài ... fùjìn...	near ...	located ... near
hútòng	hútòng	hutong
měi jǐng	nice views	beautiful view
yǒudiǎn wúliáo	a little boring	has little boring
tuǒxié	compromise	compromise
ránhòu	then	then
hǎo jìhuà	good idea	good idea

1 Find the comparison words and adjectives in the phrase list, then write them down here.

   a better _____

   b all _____

   c extremely _____

2 In the dialogue, Xiǎowēi says that the Forbidden City is more interesting and more beautiful. What are these words in Chinese?

    a interesting _____

    b beautiful _____

3 To say something is more interesting or beautiful, you add **gèng** before. For example, 'better' (or 'more good') is **gèng hǎo**. Based on this, how would you say these phrases?

    a more positive (**jījí**) _____ _____

    b more beautiful _____ _____

    c more interesting _____ _____

4 How would you write the following in Chinese?

    a I think _____ _____

    b I think soup is better. _____ _____

    c I think there are a lot of people. _____ _____

5 This section expands on the vocab you can use to express your opinions. Use the phrase list as well as language you know to match each Chinese phrase to its English counterpart.

    a **Wǒ jué de**   **1** Good idea!

    b **Hǎo de**   **2** Of course!

    c **Wǒ zhīdao**   **3** That's true.

    d **Dāngrán**   **4** Okay

    e **Wǒ bù tóngyì**   **5** I think …

    f **Zhè shì zhēn de**   **6** I don't agree

    g **Hǎo zhúyì**   **7** I know

    h **Wǒ xiǎng**   **8** I would like

#LANGUAGEHACK: sound more fluent with conversation connectors

Cushion your conversations to say much more

As a beginner, when you're asked a question in Mandarin, you may be tempted to give single word answers. Do you like this book? **Xǐhuan**. How is your food? **Hǎo**.

While you may not be able to give as detailed replies in Mandarin as you'd like to (yet!), you can learn versatile phrases to use instead of brief answers.

Conversation connectors are a type of power phrase that you can tack on to nearly anything you say. You learn them once, and you can use them again and again in countless situations to help make conversations feel a lot less one-sided. For example, in Conversation 2, Xiǎowēi uses **zái wǒ kànlái** during her conversation with Lucy.

How to use conversation connectors

Good conversation connectors should be versatile. They don't need to add any extra information to the sentence, but they should expand on an otherwise short answer. For example, if someone asks you: **Nǐ jué de fànguǎn zěnmeyàng**? you could reply with: **Wǒ jué de fànguǎn hěn hǎo, nǐne**?

Here are some different conversation connectors you can use to get you started.

For giving your opinion
⋯⋗ shuō shíhuà (to tell the truth)
⋯⋗ zài wǒ kànlái (in my opinion)
⋯⋗ nǐ wǒ zhījiān (between us)
⋯⋗ jù wǒ suǒ zhī (as far as I know)
⋯⋗ yuè lái yuè (more and more)
⋯⋗ wǒ bú quèdìng, dànshì (I don't know exactly, but)
⋯⋗ jiù xiàng nǐ yǐjing zhīdào (as you may know)

For elaborating on an idea
⋯⋗ gēng zhǔnquè de shuō (to be more precise)
⋯⋗ háiyǒu (and what's more)
⋯⋗ yīncǐ (and that's why)
⋯⋗ jiùshì shuō (that's to say)
⋯⋗ suīrán (even though)

For changing the subject

···} **lìng yì fāngmiàn** (on the other hand)

···} **shùnbiàn gēn nǐ shuō yíxià** (by the way)

Here are a few more examples of how to use conversation connectors.

→ If someone asks **Nǐ duō dà suìshu?** (How old are you?), you could say: **Wǒ 41 suì**, or:

    Nà ... jīnnián ... nǐ wǒ zhījiān ... shuō shíhuà ... 41 suì.

→ If someone asks, **Nǐ wèishénme xué Zhōngwén?** (Why are you learning Chinese?), you could say, **Wǒ jué de Zhōngguó wénhuà hěn yǒu yìsi** (I think Chinese culture is very interesting) or: **Zài wǒ kànlái Zhōngguó wénhuà hěn yǒu yìsi. Yīncǐ wǒ xué Zhōngwén**. (In my opinion, Chinese culture is very interesting. And that's why I'm studying Chinese.)

Conversation connectors help you expand on your answers and give them a much chattier feel! For beginners, momentum helps conversations stay alive better with more words.

YOUR TURN: use the Hack

Use the conversation connectors suggested to give lengthier replies to common questions.

Example: Zhè fángzi xiǎo ma? (Is this house small?)

Shuō shíhuà, wǒ jué de zhè fángzi hěn dà!

a **Nǐ de wǎncān zěnmeyàng?** (How is your food?)

_____

_____

b **Nǐ zhù zài nǎli?** (Where do you live?)

_____

_____

c **Nǐ xūyào chāoshì de shénme dōngxi ma?** (Would you like something from the market?)

_____

_____

d **Nǐ hē kāfēi ma?** (Do you drink coffee?)

_____

_____

GRAMMAR EXPLANATION: comparisons

Hopefully you're starting to see that Chinese makes it very easy to compare things!

Not as

You can say 'not as' by using **méiyǒu** – yes! That's the same **méiyǒu** as 'doesn't have'. In the dialogue, you saw this structure at work in the sentence:

Gùgōng méiyóu Chángchéng rén duō, dànshì Gùgōng méiyóu Chángchéng de měijīng.
(The Forbidden City is not as crowded as the Great Wall, but the Forbidden City's views are not as pretty as the Great Wall's.) Or literally: 'The Forbidden City doesn't have the Great Wall's people, but the Forbidden City doesn't have the Great Wall's pretty views'.

Even more

If you want to say something is 'even more', you can do this by simply adding **gèng** before the quality that you're discussing. In the dialogue, you saw: **Gùgōng gèng yǒuyìsi.** (The Forbidden City is even more interesting.)

Same as

To express that something is the same as something else, you use **yíyàng**. Between the two things you're comparing, you include **hé** (and).

Example: Tā hé tā de dìdi yíyàng gāo. (He and his younger brother are the same height.) or (He is as tall as his younger brother.)

Simply 'the best'

If you want to say something is 'the most' or 'the X-est', you add **zuì** before the adjective. So if something is 'the best', it would be **zuì hǎo**, 'oldest' would be **zuì lǎo** and 'most beautiful' would be **zuì piàoliang**. Here are each of the comparisons in action:

Not as	Even more	Same as	The best
Zhè běn shū méiyǒu nà bù diànyǐng wúliáo. (This book is not as boring as that movie.)	Zhè běn shū gèng wúliáo. (This book is even more boring.)	Zhè běn shū hé nà bù diànyǐng yíyàng wúliáo. (This book is as boring as that movie.)	Zhè běn shū zuì wúliáo. (This book is the most boring.)

PRACTICE

1 Practice forming comparisons in Chinese using the adjectives in the box.

Example: *He isn't as smart as his brother.* ———► **Tā méiyǒu tā de gēge cōngming.**

ǎi (short)	**gāo** (tall)	**cōngming** (smart)	**lèi** (tired)	**gāoxìng** (happy)
shīwàng (disappointed)	**piàoliang** (pretty)	**chǒu** (ugly)	**chòu** (smelly)	**lǎo** (old)

a My book is not as old as your book.

_____

_____

Pay special note to the tones used in **chǒu** and chòu. The tone used is what determines the difference between 'ugly' and 'smelly'.

b I am not as disappointed as her.

_____

_____

c My little sister is not as tall as my older sister.

_____

_____

d I think I am not as pretty as my mother.

_____

_____

e I am not as smart as my younger brother.

_____

_____

2 Use all the comparison words you learned to translate these sentences

a most smart/smartest

_____

_____

b Shanghai is as beautiful as Beijing.

_____

_____

c even more tired

_____

_____

3 Fill in the missing words.

a **Nánhái** _____ **nǚhái xiǎo.** (The boy is not as small as the girl.)

b **Nà shì** _____ **xiǎo de lǎoshǔ.** (That is the smallest mouse.)

c **Wǒ de shū hé tā de shū** _____ **xiǎo.** (My book is as small as hers.)

d **Wǒ de érzi** _____ **xiǎo.** (My son is more small.)

PUT IT TOGETHER

1 Where do you want to go? Recommend to a friend some things to do in a city you know or would like to visit. Use the vocab you learned in Conversation 2, as well as any new 'me-specific' vocab that you look up on your own. Try to include:

⋯⋗ the places you would like to visit (**yào qù**)
⋯⋗ the sites or experiences you think would be the best
⋯⋗ phrases for comparison
⋯⋗ phrases for expressing your opinion.

COMPLETING UNIT 6

Check your understanding

Listen to the audio, which will play sets of two statements in Mandarin. The first statement will give you information about somewhere, and the second attempts to summarize that information.

🔊 06.06 Based on what you understand, select **duì** if the summary is correct or **cuò** if it's false. Listen to the example first.

Example: Claire jué de Shànghǎi hěn dà.　　　　　　（duì）/ cuò

  a Julie jué de tàijíquán méiyǒu gōngfu yǒu yìsi.　　　duì / cuò

  b Tā jué de bówùguān bù hǎowán.　　　　　　　　duì / cuò

  c Alice yào Laura qù Táiwān, yīnwéi Táiwān
      shuǐguǒ (fruit) zuì hǎochī.　　　　　　　　　duì / cuò

MORE CHINESE CHARACTERS

In this unit, you'll learn the Chinese characters for several commonly used radicals. You'll often see these radicals as a part of other characters, and knowing what they mean will help you figure out the meaning of the character they're a part of.

口 kǒu

The character for 'mouth' is 口 and on its own, it's pronounced **kǒu**. It's a simple character with three strokes and as a radical, you'll see it in words like 听 (to listen), 吃 (to eat) and 吵 (noisy). The strokes are drawn in the following order:

口 kǒu
(3 strokes)

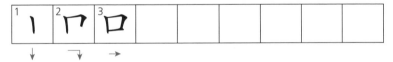

Practice writing this character in the space below.

草 cǎo

The Chinese character for 'grass' 草 includes the ⺿ radical at its top. It is often used in words for vegetables or other greenery such as 花 (flower), 菜 (dish) and 蔬菜 (vegetable). When it appears as a radical it is changed to ⺿.

As an independent character, it has nine strokes. They are written in this order:

 cǎo
(9 strokes)

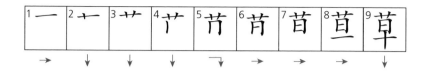

Practice writing this character in the space below.

水 shuǐ

The character for 'water' is an important character to learn because it's one you'll see and use often. It is used on its own for 'water', but can also be seen as 氵 in words like 海洋 (ocean), 港口 (harbor) or 果汁 (juice).

The character for 'water' is written with four strokes. They are written in this order:

 shuǐ
(4 strokes)

Practice writing this character in the space below.

手 shǒu

The last character you'll learn in this unit is the character for 'hand' in Chinese.

The character for 'hand' is written in four strokes. When it appears as a radical, it's squeezed horizontally and has one less stroke 扌. Some words you may see it in include 指 (to point), 拥抱 (to hug) and 按 (to press).

In character form, the strokes are drawn in this order:

手 shǒu
(4 strokes)

| 1 ㇒ | 2 二 | 3 三 | 4 手 | | | | |

Practice writing this character in the space below.

COMPLETE YOUR MISSION

It's time to complete your mission: convince your friend to try out your favorite restaurant. You'll need to prepare phrases for giving your opinions and explaining why you agree or disagree. Describe a restaurant you know and love, or research some restaurants in a Mandarin-speaking country you want to visit.

LEARNING STRATEGY: *action research*
You can see how Mandarin speakers in real life describe their favorite (or least favorite) restaurant experiences by reading their own words … online! Read restaurant reviews in Chinese online to help you form your argument. Get more details on adding this step to your mission by going online to the #LanguageHacking community.

STEP 1: build your script
Keep building your script! Use opinion phrases and me-specific vocab to:

···❯ describe your favorite restaurant. Say what type of food and drinks they serve. Why do you like it so much? Which are your favorite dishes and why?
···❯ convince a friend to try it out by saying what makes it better than other restaurants in town (use comparisons)
···❯ give or ask for a recommendation
···❯ include power phrases and conversation connectors.
···❯ Write down your script, then repeat it until you feel confident.

Yes, it is! Personalize your language to talk about yourself and what's important to you! Learning a language is easier when you can talk about things that are meaningful!

STEP 2: it's all about me! … online
When you feel good about your script, go online to find your next mission and share your recording with the community. This time, as you're speaking, use conversation connectors between phrases and while you're thinking to help your Mandarin flow better. By using these phrases right away, you'll also start burning them into your muscle memory, so they are at the tip of your tongue when you need them.

STEP 3: learn from other learners

Test out your debate skills with other language hackers! Your task is to reply in Mandarin to at least three different people to tell them whether you agree or disagree with the argument they made and why. Use the phrases **Nǐ shuō de duì** and **Wǒ míngbai** to let them know that you understand their point of view.

STEP 4: reflect on what you learned

What did you find easy or difficult about this unit? Did you learn any new words or phrases in the community space? After every script you write or conversation you have, you'll gain lots of insight for what words you need to fill in your script.

HEY, LANGUAGE HACKER, LOOK AT YOU GO!

Now you can share opinions, talk about food, make comparisons and keep the conversation flowing – you've come a long way. Cherish this feeling and know that things can only improve from here!

Next, let's make a huge leap forward with the range of conversations you can have – by starting to talk about the past.

Jiāyóu! (Go for it!)

NOTES

7 TALKING ABOUT YESTERDAY...
LAST WEEK ... A LONG TIME AGO

Mission

Imagine this – you've just joined a Mandarin-speaking meet-up group and you have to introduce yourself by sharing personal stories, but with a twist – it can be true or completely made up.

Your mission is to tell a true, but possibly unbelievable story, or one completely made-up story in as convincing a way as possible. Be prepared to describe a personal story or a life lesson you've learned from past experiences, whether in learning a new language, moving to a new place, or taking a big risk.

This mission will help you expand the range of conversation topics you can confidently contribute to and allow you to use anecdotes to spice up your Mandarin repertoire.

Mission prep:

···⟩ Discuss completed actions with verbal complements: dào, wán, bǎo, jiàn
···⟩ Talk about the past in two steps: Guo ... le
···⟩ Answer questions about the past week or weekends using: shàng and xià
···⟩ Say how long ago something happened using: qián
···⟩ Use the past tense to talk about your progress in Chinese: le and guò

BUILDING LANGUAGE FOR RICHER CONVERSATIONS

The range of what you can discuss in Mandarin has until now focused on what's happening now or in the future. By the end of this unit, you'll be able to give detailed descriptions of things you did in the past, which will help you have much richer conversations.

#LANGUAGEHACK:
time travel – talk about the past and future using the present

CONVERSATION 1

What did you do last weekend?

As you make friends with other Mandarin speakers, or practice with the same people regularly, a big question is often 'What am I going to talk about?' Being able to use and understand the Chinese past tense is a great solution to this problem. You can use it to describe personal stories about your life, which makes for endless conversation topics.

Lucy is talking again with Jùnfēng, one of her online teachers.

🔊 **07.01** How does Jùnfēng ask, 'What did you do last weekend?'

> **Jùnfēng :** Lucy, nǐ hǎo! Nǐ zuìjìn zěnmeyàng? Nǐ shàng zhōumò zuò shénme le?
>
> **Lucy :** Xiǎowěi hé wǒ yìqǐ chūqù wán le … Wǒmen yě tǎolùn le wǒmen zhōumò de jìhuà. Zuótiān wǒmen kàndào le Chángchéng … Wǒmen pāi le hěnduō zhàopiàn!
>
> **Jùnfēng :** Zěnmeyàng? Hǎowán ma?
>
> **Lucy :** Hěn hǎowán! Xiǎowěi duì lìshǐ hé zhèngzhì zhīdao hěn duō. Wǒmen de huìhuà hěn yǒu yìsi. Qù Chángchéng yǐhòu, wǒmen yòu cānguān le Gùgōng.
>
> **Jùnfēng :** Nǐmen zhǐ rènshi le yí ge xīngqī, duì bu duì?
>
> **Lucy :** Duì.
>
> **Jùnfēng :** Sì nián qián, wo qù guo Chángchéng.
>
> **Lucy :** Xǐhuan ma?
>
> **Jùnfēng :** Hái kěyǐ … Wǒ tèbié xǐhuan Chángchéng de fànguǎn. Zài nàli, wǒ shì yí ge rén chī le yì pán lǎo cù huāshēng.

FIGURE IT OUT

1 Look for these phrases in the conversation and highlight them.

a Jùnfēng asks about what Lucy did last weekend. What is 'last weekend' in Chinese?

_____

_____

b Lucy shares that she and Xiǎowěi went to see the Great Wall. She says 'Yesterday we saw …'. What is this in Chinese?

_____

_____

c How does Jùnfēng ask 'How was it?' after Lucy shares what she did?

_____

_____

d Lucy answers 'It was a lot of fun!' How do you say this in Chinese?

_____

_____

e Jùnfēng shares he went to the Great Wall in the past. What is the phrase he uses to say 'four years ago'?

_____

_____

f Jùnfēng shares what he ate when he visited the Great Wall. How does he say that he 'ate a plate of vinegar peanuts'?

_____

_____

2 What is Jùnfēng's opinion of the Great Wall? Hint: Lucy asks him if he likes it.

    a It's fun.   **b** It's okay.   **c** Didn't like it.

3 **Duì** or **cuò**? Select the correct answer.

    a Xiǎowēi and Lucy visited the Great Wall yesterday.   **duì / cuò**

    b Xiǎowēi knows a lot about history and politics.   **duì / cuò**

    c Yesterday, Lucy went to the night market.   **duì / cuò**

    d Lucy met Xiǎowēi one week ago.   **duì / cuò**

4 What do you think the phrase **yí ge rén** means in this context? It literally means 'one person', but it can also have another similar meaning which is used here.

_____

_____

5 What are the Chinese words for:

    a plans (hint: Lucy uses this word in the expression 'weekend plans'.)

    _____

    b conversation (hint: Lucy said her conversation was very interesting.)

    _____

    c especially (hint: Jùnfēng says he especially likes the restaurants at the Great Wall.) _____

NOTICE

🔊 **07.02** Listen to the audio and study the table.

Essential phrases for Conversation 1

Chinese	Meaning	Literal translation
Nǐ shàng zhōumò zuò shénme le?	What did you do last weekend?	You above weekend do what le?
cānguān le	went sightseeing	sightseeing [change particle]
tǎolùn	chat	chat
zhōumò de jìhuà	weekend plans	weekend of plans
... dào	... [completed action]	... arrive
pāi zhàopiàn	take photos	take photo
lìshǐ	history	history
zhèngzhì	politics	politics
huìhuà	conversation	conversation
cānguān	to visit/sight-see	visit
hái kěyǐ	it's okay	still can
tèbié	especially	especially
lǐ	inside	inside
yí ge rén	alone, one person	one [measure word] person
lǎo cù huāshēng	vinegar peanuts	old vinegar peanut

1 Find each example of the past in the phrase list, then write them out in Chinese.

a What did you do last weekend?

_____

_____

b Xiǎowěi and I went sight-seeing together.

_____

_____

c We also talked about our plans for the weekend.

_____

_____

2 Now highlight each of the following phrases in the Chinese sentences you wrote in Exercise 1.

a last weekend　　　**b** together　　　**c** our weekend plans

3 Use the literal translations in the phrase list to fill in the missing past tense phrases in the table. The first one has been done for you. The change of state marker **le** follows the verbs (action words) in the below.

Dictionary form	Chinese – past tense phrase	Meaning
zuò (to do/to make)	Nǐ zuò shénme le?	What did you do?
	a	We made (vinegar peanuts).
chī wǎnfàn (to eat dinner)	b	We ate dinner.
chī (to eat)	c	I ate.
shuō (to talk)	d	We talked.
kàn dào (to see to read)	e	We saw …
jiàndào (to meet)	f	You met (her)
pāi zhàopiàn (to take photos)	g	We took photos.
cānguān (to visit / to sight-see)	h	I visited …
xǐhuan (to like)	i	Did you like it?
	j	I liked it!

4 Qián (ago/before) works in that you can use it to refer to a period of time in the past, as in **sì nián qián** (four years ago). Based on this, use **qián** to complete the following sentences.

a ＿＿＿＿＿＿＿＿ ＿＿＿＿＿＿＿＿ ＿＿＿＿＿＿＿＿
nǐ zuò shénme le? (What did you do three days ago?)

b ＿＿＿＿＿＿＿＿ ＿＿＿＿＿＿＿＿ ＿＿＿＿＿＿＿＿
kàn le yì běn shū. (I read a book four days ago.)

c ＿＿＿＿＿＿＿＿ **fēnzhōng** ＿＿＿＿＿＿＿＿, **diànyǐng**
kāishǐ le. (The movie started ten minutes [**fēnzhōng**] ago.)

GRAMMAR EXPLANATION: forming the past with verbal complements

Chinese uses several forms of 'complements', words or phrases that add additional information to a verb. One form of this additional information is the expression of result.

In English, we have separate verbs to express result. For example, you look and as a result, you see. You listen, and as a result, you hear.

Here are several common verbs and complements:

Verb	Complement wán	Meaning	Complement dào	Meaning	Complement jiàn	Meaning	Complement bǎo	Meaning
chī (to eat)	chīwán	ate completely					chībǎo	ate until full
kàn (to look)	kànwán	read/watch completely	kàndào	saw	kànjiàn	see		
zuò (to do)	zuòwán	do until done	zuòdào	accomplish				
zhǎo (to look for)			zhǎodào	find				

Fill in the gaps to make a past tense sentence using completed actions with the verbs given.

a Tā _____ _____ le tā de zuòyè.
(He did his homework completely.)

b Tā _____ _____ le. (She ate until full.)

c Wǒ _____ _____ le yì běn shū. (I found a book.)

d Nǐ _____ _____ le. (You finished eating.)

e Nǐ tīng _____ shénme shēngyīn le? (What sound did you hear?)

PRACTICE

You can now create new types of full sentences! Write out in Chinese:

a The restaurant is good. I ate there two days ago.

_____
_____

b She went to Dublin with her younger brother.

_____
_____

c I read the book completely today.

_____
_____

PUT IT TOGETHER

Nǐ zuótiān/shàng zhōumò zuò shénme le?

Let's use the past forms you've just learned to create 'me-specific' sentences that you could use in real conversations. Answer the questions in Chinese with real details about your life. You might include:

⤑ what you did, what you ate.
⤑ who you saw, who you talked with.
⤑ what you talked about.

CONVERSATION 2

When did you begin learning Mandarin?

Another great way to expand your Mandarin conversations is to learn to talk about your Mandarin progress in Mandarin! People will definitely ask you these questions, so let's prepare you to answer them in Mandarin. Now that Lucy and Jùnfēng have caught up, they start discussing what Lucy has been doing to improve her Mandarin.

🔊 **07.03** How does Jùnfēng ask, 'Did you study Mandarin this week?'

Jùnfēng : Nǐ zhè ge xīngqī xué Zhōngwén le ma?

Lucy : Xué le. Xué le yìdiǎn. Wǒ xué shēngcí le. Yě gēn Xiǎowēi liànxí le jǐ ge jùzi.

Jùnfēng : Nà hǎo ba! Nǐ zuò wán zuòyè le ma?

Lucy : Zuò wán le. Gěi nǐ.

Jùnfēng : Nǐ yǒu wèntí ma?

Lucy : Yǒu. Fángzi hé jiā yǒu shénme qūbié? Wǒ de fāyīn hǎo bu hǎo?

Jùnfēng : Hǎo. Méi yǒu hěn dà de qūbié. Fángzi shì 'house', dànshì jiā shì 'home'. Ni de fāyīn hěn hǎo. Wǒ bìxū shuō, nǐ de Zhōngwén de shuǐpíng tígāo le hěn duō. Nǐ shì shénme shíhou kāishǐ xué Zhōngwén de?

Lucy : Yí ge yuè qián. Wǒ qùnián xiàtiān juédìng lǚxíng yì nián, mǎi le yì zhāng piào qù Tiānjīn. Ránhou wǒ lái le Běijīng.

Jùnfēng : Duì. Wǒ wàng le! Nǐ yǐjing gàosu wǒ le!

FIGURE IT OUT

1 Each of the following sentences are **cuò**. Highlight the words that make them incorrect and write out the correct replacements in Chinese.

a Lucy practiced one sentence with Xiǎowēi. _____

b Lucy began learning Chinese only a few weeks ago. _____

c Lucy bought a ticket to go to Xi'an. _____

2 Read the conversation and answer the questions.

a What did Lucy do with Xiǎowēi to help her with Chinese this week?

_____

_____

b What is the meaning of the phrases: **Wǒ wàng le! Nǐ yǐjing gàosu wǒ le!**

_____

_____

c What phrase does Lucy use to check her pronunciation **(fāyīn)**?

_____

_____

3 Use context to figure out the meaning of these words/phrases.

a qūbié _____

b wǒ juédìng _____

c zuòyè _____

NOTICE

🔊 **07.04** Listen to the audio and study the table.

Essential phrases for Conversation 2

Chinese	Meaning	Literal translation
shēngcí	new words	new word
jǐ ge jùzi	a few sentences	some [measure word] sentence
Nǐ zuò wán zuòyè le ma?	Did you finish your homework?	You do finish homework [change marker] [question marker]?
Gěi nǐ.	Here it is.	Give you.
fángzi	house	house
jiā	home	home
qūbié	difference	difference
fāyīn	pronunciation	pronunciation
Wǒ bìxū shuō ...	I must say ...	I must speak ...
shuǐpíng	level	level
tígāo	improve	improve
juédìng	decide	decide
qùnián xiàtiān	last summer	last year summer
mǎi yì zhāng piào	buy a ticket	buy one [measure word for flat objects] ticket
Wǒ wàng le!	I forgot!	I forget [change marker]!

1 Find these power phrases in the phrase list, and write them out in Chinese.

a I must say ... _____ _____

b I forgot! _____ _____

c Did you finish ...? _____ _____

2 There's a new measure word in the phrase list. Which is it? Hint: it's used to measure a ticket. _____

3 Use the phrase list below to help you recognize the past tense phrases in Chinese. Choose the word or phrase from the list, then write it out next to its English counterpart.

xué dào le	qù guo	zuò wán le	tīng dào le
zuò hǎo le	lái guo	chī le	mǎi le

a learned _____ **e** bought _____

b came _____ **f** went _____

c finished _____ **g** studied _____

d heard _____ **h** ate _____

GRAMMAR EXPLANATION: using guo for experiences

When using **guo** in the past tense, you're discussing something you experienced in the past.

If you ate today, you may not want to refer to what you had in particular, so you might use **chī le**. But if you are discussing having the experience of eating something specific, like vinegar peanuts or a meal, you would use **chī guo**.

Here are a few examples:

Nǐ xué guo Zhōngwén ma? ⟶ Have you had the experience of studying Chinese? / Have you ever studied Chinese?

Nǐ kàn guo zhè ge diànshì jiémù ma? ⟶ Have you had the experience of watching this TV show? / Have you ever seen this TV show?

Nǐ qù guo Běijīng ma? ⟶ Have you been to Beijing? / Have you ever been to Beijing before?

Hint: If you would use 'have you ever' in English, or if you're talking about an experience, use **guo** in Chinese.

Using guo with le

Both **guo** and **le** can be used on their own to indicate something that happened in the past. They can also be used together to describe habitual actions like showering or brushing your teeth. In this structure, **guo** follows the verb and **le** goes at the end of the sentence.

Example: Wŏ yĭjing shuā guo yá le. ⟶ I already brushed my teeth.

1 Try it! Use **guo + le** to form the past tense phrase for 'He already ate.'

_____

_____

2 Fill in the gaps with the past tense using **guo** or **le**, and pay attention to the word order you use.

a Sān ge yuè qián, wŏ qù _____ Jiānádà.
(Three months ago I traveled to Canada. [Hint: it's an experience!])

b Nĭ jīntiān chī _____ _____ ma?
(Have you eaten today?)

c Zhèli yŏu yì bĕn shū. Nĭ kànjiàn _____ ma?
(There's a book here. Did you see it?)

3 Use what you've learned about the past tense to fill in Sections 1 and 2 of the past tense cheat sheet with key verbs in Chinese. (Leave the rest of the cheat sheet blank for now.)

PAST TENSE CHEAT SHEET

1 Verbs	Past form	2 Verbs	Past experience	3 Me-specific verbs	Past forms (both past and past experience forms)
I spoke	shuō le	I spoke	shuō guo	Example: I drank	hē guo le
I made		I made			
I bought		I bought			
I came		I came			
I studied		I studied			
I saw		I saw			
I ate		I ate			

PUT IT TOGETHER

1 Use the past tense to describe the details of a trip you took to another city. Draw from your own experiences to create sentences that answer the questions:

⋯⟩ **Nǐ shì shénme shíhou lái de?**

⋯⟩ **Nǐ wèishénme juédìng qù …?**

⋯⟩ **Nǐ xǐhuan ma? Wèishénme?**

2 Imagine you're having a conversation with someone in Mandarin, when you casually mention an interesting anecdote and the other person says, **Tài niú le! Nǐ zuò le shénme?** (Cool! What did you do?)

Answer the question with detailed sentences about a time in your life. You could write about somewhere you went, a film you saw, or anything else – but try to use new verbs you haven't used before. Try to include several past-tense verbs in various forms to describe:

⋯⟩ specific details of what happened – who did what?

⋯⟩ specific details of conversations – who said what?

⋯⟩ where you went, when you returned.

 #LANGUAGEHACK: time travel – talk about the past and future using the present

Language learning is a process, and as a beginner Chinese learner, it's important to remember that you don't need to learn everything at once!

One of the truly fun aspects of languages is how flexible, fluid and creative they can be! Let's explore this one now, by figuring out how many inventive ways you can express yourself in the past, even if you don't think you have the grammar or vocab for it yet.

Use time words

This is an easy way to form the past tense in Chinese, and also the clearest. Some of the most common past words include **yǐ qián** (before), **shàng zhōu** (last week), **zuótiān** (yesterday) and **gānggāng** (only just). If you want to make sure it's clear that you're discussing something in the past, just include the time when it happened.

Use time indicators to travel through time

When you learned booster verbs, you saw that **wǒ yào** can be used for 'I will' or 'I want to' to indicate something happening in the future. But a handy alternative that's also used frequently to refer to a future event is to use a time indicator!

Tell a story!

Once you've learned to use time indicators, you can build on them to form the past through 'storytelling'. For example, have you ever told a story that went something like this?

'So the other day, there I am ... minding my own business, when someone comes up to me, and you'll never guess what happens!'

Though it's clearly an anecdote about something that happened in the past, the entire sentence actually uses present tense forms – 'there I am', 'someone comes up to me'. You can do the same thing in Chinese! To make this narrative style work, you just need to:

give details that set the context of the situation to make it clear that it's a story. You can use time indicators, but other details work as well – say where you are, when it's happening or what you're doing then simply say what happened, using the present form!

Examples: Shàng ge xīngqī yī, wǒ zhèngzài chī zuìhǎo de Běijīng kǎoyā ...

(Last Monday, I'm in the middle of eating the best Beijing duck ...)

Suǒyǐ wǒ zài yèshì, zhèngzài mǎi chòu dòufu ...

(So I'm at the night market, in the middle of buying stinky tofu ...)

Just say it 'Tarzan' style

If all else fails, the world won't end if all you can think of is the basic words and not the grammar. Though you will want to use this sparingly, people will get the gist of what you're saying even if all you can get is something like:

Zuótiān ... fànguǎn ... chī pīsà. (Yesterday ... restaurant ... eat pizza.)
Always remember that saying something badly is miles better than saying nothing at all. And in fact, it's an opportunity to get corrections from a helpful Chinese speaker!

I recommend you focus on improving one major aspect of your language skills at a time. Start with the most important ones first, then fine tune from there. Remember, people will see that you're a beginner and they will forgive the error!

YOUR TURN: use the hack

1 Use time indicators to say in Chinese:

    a I watch the movie now.

    _____

    _____

    b I will watch the movie tomorrow.

    _____

    _____

    c I watched the movie last week.

    _____

    _____

2 How would you attempt to tell the following implied story if you couldn't think of the grammar for these phrase chunks?

Sān tiān qián … zuò huǒchē (on the train) **… kàn jiàn … yì zhī láng** (a wolf) **…**

    _____

    _____

3 Create 'me-specific' sentences in which you describe things you did at different time periods.

    a a week ago _____   b last Saturday _____

    c two years ago _____   d yesterday _____

    Now say what you are going to do:

    e next (**xià**) Wednesday _____ _____

    f next (**míng**) year _____ _____

PUT IT TOGETHER

1 Tell a story about a time you got nervous speaking Mandarin. Using what you've learned, describe those moments – what you were thinking, doing, saying and what you learned. Be sure to include:

  ⋯⟩ at least three of the following verbs: **jué de**, **shuō**, **xuédào**, **zuò**, **wàng**, in the past

  ⋯⟩ a specific time indicator (**shàng zhōumò …**)

  ⋯⟩ details of what you did to overcome your nerves (**Wǒ juédìng mànman shuō…**).

COMPLETING UNIT 7

Check your understanding

Feel free to take notes or listen to it multiple times.

1 🔊 **07.05** Listen to this audio rehearsal first, in which a Mandarin speaker describes meeting Mark, a tourist visiting Beijing.

Shàng zhōu mò, wǒ zài shàngbān. Wǒ zài yì jiā fànguǎn gōngzuò. Yí ge rén lái le. Wǒ wèn tā, 'jǐ wèi?' Tā gàosu wǒ, 'wǒ shì yí ge rén'. Yīnwèi tā shì yí ge rén, wǒ juédìng gēn tā liáotiān. Tā gàosu wǒ tā shì Měiguórén, dànshì xiànzài zhù zài Fǎguó. Tā huì shuō Fǎyǔ. Tā yǒu liǎng ge háizi.

2 🔊 **07.06** Now listen to the second audio, which will ask you questions about Mark. Answer them out loud in Mandarin.

   a Mark yǒu háizi ma?

   b Mark shì hé péngyou yīqǐ lái de ma?

   c Ta xiànzài zhù zài nǎli?

   d Mark shì nǎ guó rén?

MORE CHINESE CHARACTERS

In this unit, you'll learn more common radicals.

火 *huǒ*

The character for 'fire' is 火 and on its own, it's pronounced **huǒ**. Doesn't it look like a bonfire? It has four strokes and as a radical, you'll see it in words like 灯 (lamp) and 烧 (burn). The strokes are drawn in the following order:

火 huǒ (4 strokes)

1 丶	2 丷	3 少	4 火				

Practice writing this character in the space below.

日 rì

The Chinese character for 'sun' is often used as a radical in words related to time or the weather such as 时 (time) and 晴 (sunny).

As for character, it has four strokes. They are written in this order:

Practice writing this character in the space below.

月 yuè

The character for 'moon' is an important character to learn because it's used alone as a character to mean both 'moon' and 'month', as well as the radical component in many words. It can be seen in words like 明 (tomorrow) and 服 (clothes).

The character for 'moon' is written with four strokes. They are written in this order:

Practice writing this character in the space below.

土 tǔ

The last character you'll learn in this unit is the character for 'earth' in Chinese.

The character for 'earth' is written in three strokes. When it appears as a radical, it's squeezed horizontally, and the bottom stroke tilts up and to the right as you'll see in words like 地 (earth).

In character form, the strokes are drawn in this order:

¹一	²十	³土				
→	↓	→				

Practice writing this character in the space below.

Show what you know...

Here's what you've just learned. Write or say an example for each item in the list. Then check off the ones you know.

- ☐ Say the past tense phrases: I ate, I said, I went, I learned, I saw
- ☐ Give a sentence using **qián** to say how long ago you did something.
- ☐ Give time indicators for: 'yesterday' and 'last weekend', 'last week' and 'tomorrow'.

COMPLETE YOUR MISSION

It's time to complete your mission: put on your poker face and start your story. Try to fool the language-hacking community as best you can.

STEP 1: build your script

Wǒ shuō le ... Wǒ tīng dào le ...

Expand on your scripts by using 'me-specific' vocab to describe an important life lesson you gained from a past experience. Be sure to include:

···⟩ time indicators to describe when this happened (**qián**)

···⟩ several past tense verbs in various forms to describe what you thought, what you wanted, what you learned and more

···⟩ as many details as possible! (Use the time travel #languagehack if you get stuck.)

Write down your script, then repeat it until you feel confident.

STEP 2: don't be a wallflower. Use language in real social contexts ... online

If you're feeling good about your script, it's time to complete your mission. Go online to find your mission for Unit 7 and share your recording.

STEP 3: earn from other learners

Your task is to watch at least two video clips uploaded by other hackers. Then ask three follow-up questions in Mandarin to see if they can keep the conversation going, to help them fill the gaps in their scripts, and to figure out whether what they say is **duì** or **cuò**. Make your guess.

STEP 4: reflect on what you learned

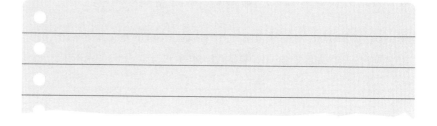

HEY, LANGUAGE HACKER, SEE HOW THINGS HAVE CHANGED?

You've just learned how to talk about anything in the past. Now you can reminisce on the long-forgotten days when you couldn't speak Mandarin.

Next, you'll add even more detail to your conversations by describing the specific parts of your daily routine.

Nǐ shuō de fēicháng hǎo!

8 IT'S BEEN A WHILE!

Mission

Imagine this – one of your Mandarin-speaking friends runs a vlog about the daily routines of highly productive people – like you – and you've been asked to contribute a vlog clip!

Your mission is to prepare your best productivity advice – in Mandarin – for the blog. Be prepared to describe your daily routine from your first morning beverage to your bedtime. Talk about what works well and what you'd like to be different.

This mission will broaden your ability to discuss your daily life and help you become comfortable with small talk in Mandarin.

Mission prep:

⋯⟩ Talk about your hobbies, routines and daily life.
⋯⟩ Use versatile phrases to express your opinions and perceptions.
⋯⟩ Use phrases for seeing people you know again: **Hǎojiǔ bú jiàn! / Zuìjìn hái hǎo ma?**
⋯⟩ Build upon modes of transport.
⋯⟩ Talk about what you would potentially do: **wǒ kěnéng.**

BUILDING LANGUAGE FOR DESCRIBING YOUR DAILY LIFE

As a beginner Chinese learner, it's difficult to be very detailed when you speak, so your energy is often best spent learning phrases that express a general idea of what you're trying to say.

But now, you're quickly becoming an upper-beginner Chinese learner! So it's time to learn some tricks for adding more detail to your conversations without a huge amount of new vocab. In this unit, we'll break a typical conversation into its component parts to develop a more complex strategy for helping each part flow well.

#LANGUAGEHACK:
the rephrasing technique for talking your way through complicated sentences

CONVERSATION 1

It's been a while!

You don't have to think it up on the spot – instead, prepare in advance with strategic phrases you can use to initiate, warm up and extend any conversation.

When a conversation has passed the point of usual pleasantries, where should you go from there?

🔊 08.01 Lucy and Wǎntíng are meeting for lunch at a café. Since they already know each other, they can't rely on the usual meet-and-greet expressions. What phrases do Lucy and Wǎntíng use to 'warm up' the conversation?

CULTURE TIP: *Chinese cuisine*
There are said to be 'Eight Cuisines of China' – Anhui, Cantonese, Fujian, Hunan, Jiangsu, Shandong, Sichuan and Zhejiang. They can be very different in style, flavor and ingredients, and it's worth exploring each style if you have the chance. **Nǎihuáng bāo** are a custard - filled pastry particularly popular in Cantonese cuisine. **Jiǎozi** are a dumpling filled with minced meat and vegetables popular all across China.

Wǎntíng : Lucy, nǐ hǎo! Hǎojiǔ bú jiàn!

Lucy : Duì. Zuìjìn hái hǎo ma?

Wǎntíng : Hěn hǎo. Tīng de chūlái, nǐ de Zhōngwén gèng hǎo le. Suǒyǐ, gàosu wǒ ba, zuìjìn máng bu máng?

Lucy : Nà … xiànzài yǒudiǎn máng. Zuìjìn wǒ gānggāng kāishǐ xué zěnme zuòfàn. Wǒ měi ge xīngqī yǒu yì jié kè.

Wǎntíng : Zhēn de? Nǐ xiànzài zhèngzài xué zuò shénme?

Lucy : Shàngcì wǒmen xué le zěnme zuò **nǎihuáng bāo**. Shàngkè de shíhou, kànqǐlái dōu hěn jiǎndān, dànshì, zài jiā wǒ yí ge rén zuò hái méiyǒu chénggōng guo.

Wǎntíng : Hěn yǒu yìsi. Wǒ méiyǒu yíyàng de wèntí … Wǒ de wēibōlú pīsà zǒngshì fēicháng hǎochī. Wǒ rènzhēn yìdiǎn … jìxù ba. Zhè zhǐ shì shíjiān wèntí. Jìxù liànxí. Liànxí hěn zhòngyào.

Lucy : Wǒ zhīdao! Wǒ xué de hěn kuài. Wǒ xiànzài zhèngzài xué zěnme zuò jiǎozi!

FIGURE IT OUT

1 Highlight the phrases in which Lucy says:

    a she goes to her **kè** (class) once a week.

    b what she and her classmates learned to make **shàng cì** (last time).

    c what she **xiànzài zhèngzài xué** (is currently learning) to make.

2 Use what you understood to fill in the missing details in English.

    a Wǎntíng thinks that Lucy's Chinese has gotten _____ _____.

    b At home, Lucy still **hái méiyǒu** (hasn't) _____.

    c Wǎntíng jokes that her _____ is **zǒngshì fēicháng hǎochī** (always very good).

3 Use context to figure out how the speakers say 'Long time no see!'

_____

_____

4 Answer these questions, giving your answers in Chinese.

    a Lucy zuìjìn kāishǐ zuò shénme le?

    _____

    _____

    b Xiànzài Lucy zhèngzài xué zuò shénme cài?

    _____

    _____

5 Highlight the following Chinese phrases in the conversation and write them below:

    a When Wǎntíng tells Lucy her Chinese has gotten better, she starts the statement with 'I hear', what is this in Chinese?

    _____

    _____

    b After Wǎntíng tells Lucy her Chinese is better, she asks 'Have you been busy lately?' Find and write this question:

    _____

    _____

    c When Lucy shares the problem she is having, Wǎntíng tells her, 'I don't have the same problem.' How do you say this in Chinese?

    _____

    _____

NOTICE

🔊 08.02 Listen to the audio and study the table.

Chinese	Meaning	Literal translation
Hǎojiǔ bú jiàn!	Long time no see!	Long time not see!
Zuìjìn hái hǎo ma?	Have you been good lately?	Lately still good [question marker]?
tīng de chūlái	heard	hear of come
gèng hǎo	even better	even more good
Zuìjìn máng bu máng?	Have you been busy lately?	Lately busy not busy?
Wǒ gānggāng kāishǐ xué zěnme ...	I just started to study how to ...	I just start study how ...
Wǒ měi ge xīngqī yǒu yì jié kè.	I have a class every week.	I every [measure word] week have one [measure word] class.
zhèngzài ...	in the middle of ...	in the middle of ...
shàngcì	last time	above time
nǎihuáng bāo	custard - filled pastry	milk yellow bun
shàngkè de shíhou	during the last class	above class of time
kànqǐlái dōu hěn jiǎndān	it seems like everything is simple	look rise come all very simple
wǒ yí ge rén hái méiyǒu chénggōng guo	I haven't succeeded on my own	I one [measure word] person still not have succeed
yíyàng de wèntí	the same problem	same of problem
wēibōlú pīsà zǒngshì fēicháng hǎo chī	microwave pizza is always extremely tasty	microwave pizza always extremely good eat
Wǒ rènzhēn yìdiǎn ...	I'll be serious ...	I serious a little ...
Jìxù liànxí.	Keep practicing.	Continue practice.
zhòngyào	important	important

1 What two phrases can you use to greet someone you haven't seen in a while? Hint: one is a question!

_____   _____

_____   _____

As well as 'to do', zuò also means 'to make'. Hěn yǒuyòng! (Very useful!)

2 Notice how Chinese expresses these phrases. Write them out, using the literal translations in the phrase list to help you.

a I just started _____   **b** in the middle of _____

c recently _____   **e** last time _____

d a little busy _____   **f** it seems like _____

3 Use the phrase list to fill in the gaps in each expression.

a **Nǐ** _____ _____ **xué zuò shénme?**
(What are you learning to make at the moment?)

b **Wǒ xué de** _____ _____ (I learn quickly.)

c _____ _____ **wǒ yí ge rén zuò hái méiyǒu chénggōng guo.** (I haven't succeeded at home alone yet.)

d **Zhè zhǐ shì** _____ _____ (It's only a matter of time.)

4 Determine which word is missing from each of the sentences.

a **Chī de** _____ **hěn zhòngyào.** (It's important to eat well.)

b **Wǒ de péngyou** _____ **xué jiànzhù le.** (My friend started studying architecture.)

c **Zài jiā** _____ **fàn bǐjiào jiànkāng.** (It's healthier to cook food at home.)

5 Notice the Chinese phrase for 'I learned how to make' and 'I'm in the middle of learning how to'. Based on this, fill in the gaps to say the following in Chinese.

a **Nǐ** _____ _____ **dàngāo?** (How do you make cake?)

b **Wǒmen** _____ _____ _____

tiàowǔ. (We're in the middle of learning how to dance.)

c **Qùnián, wǒ** _____ _____ _____
zěnme dú hànzì. (Last year, I learned how to read Chinese characters.)

GRAMMAR TIP:
how to
In English, when you express that you're learning something, you might say you're learning 'how to' do that thing. So, for example, you wouldn't say you're 'learning to cook', but 'learning how to cook'. The same is true in Chinese: **xuéxí zěnme zuòfàn** (learning how to cook). Or **gàosu wǒ zěnme zuò** (tell me how to do it). And **wǒ zhīdao zěnme shuō** (I know how to say it).

GRAMMAR TIP:
in the middle of
Earlier, you learned how to talk about things you did in the past by adding **guo** and **le**. You're now learning how to talk about what you're doing presently. In Chinese, this is easy to do! You simply add **zhèngzài** before the action word. Here are a couple of examples:

Wǒ xuéxí Hányǔ.   I am learning Korean. (general statement)
Wǒ zhèngzài xuéxí Hányǔ.   I am in the middle of/in the process of learning Korean.

Wǒ měitiān zuò wǎnfàn.   I make dinner every day.
Wǒ zhèngzài zuò wǎnfàn.   I am in the middle of making dinner.

CONVERSATION STRATEGY: learn set phrases for each 'stage' of a conversation

A lot of people get nervous about what to say during a conversation. If you're meeting someone for the first time, it's easy – just introduce yourself. But if you've talked before, or you've finished your greetings, you'll need to keep the conversation going. When you understand the structure of a typical conversation, you can break it down into its component parts and prepare phrases to use at the different stages in a conversation. This way, you're never stuck wondering what to say next.

Warm up the conversation
During the first few seconds of a conversation, use some longer pleasantries to give yourself time to collect your thoughts. For example:
⋯⟩ **Hǎojiǔ bú jiàn!** (Long time no see!)
⋯⟩ **Wǒ hěn gāoxìng kàn dào nǐ!** (I'm happy to see you!)

Get the conversation started
Set a conversation topic into motion! Prepare phrases to get the other person talking for a few minutes:
⋯⟩ **Gàosu wǒ ba, zuìjìn nǐ zěnmeyàng?** (Tell me, how have things been lately?)
⋯⟩ **Kànqǐlái nǐ hěn lèi/gāoxìng/shāngxīn.** (You seem tired/happy/sad.)

Lead the conversation yourself
When it's again your turn to talk, think of some phrases you can use to lead the discussion on your own and introduce a new conversation topic.
⋯⟩ **Zuìjìn wǒ gānggāng kāishǐ ...** (Well, lately I started ...)
⋯⟩ **... xīn gōngzuò** (a new job) **... xué zěnme zuòfàn** (to learn how to cook), etc.
⋯⟩ **Zuìjìn wǒ ...** (Lately I've ...)

Extend the conversation
Show your interest with filler words like **hěn yǒu yìsi** and **zhēn de ma**? But a slightly more detailed question, prepared in advance, will urge the other person to expand on the topic, and therefore extend the conversation. For example:
⋯⟩ **Nǐ jué de zěnmeyàng?** (What do you think?)
⋯⟩ **Hǎowán ma?** (Is it fun?)

Add detail to your conversations

Remember that you can get more out of a conversation by expanding on a topic with details about when, where or how something happened. For example, to describe recent travels, you could say **Wǒ jīngcháng yīnwèi gōngzuò chūchāi**. (I travel often for my work.) But why not go on to elaborate on this by adding descriptive details (when? what?):

⋯⟿ **Zuìhòu yícì** (last time) ... **fēi le bā ge xiǎoshí** (I flew for eight hours)

⋯⟿ **Cānjiā yí ge huìyì** (I attended a conference) ... **zài Jiānádà** (in Canada)

Study the table and see how a conversation can flow:

Language hacker A	Language hacker B
Conversational warmers	**Conversational warmers**
Hǎojiǔ bújiàn!	Xièxie nǐ / Xièxie nǐ de ...
Wǒ hěn gāoxìng kàn dào nǐ!	
Conversational starters	**Starting replies**
Gàosu wǒ ba, zuìjìn nǐ zěnmeyàng?	Hái hǎo, yíqiè dōu hěn hǎo.
Nǐ hái hǎo ma?	**Conversation leads**
Kàn qǐlái ... (nǐ yǒu yí ge xīn péngyou ...)	Zuìjìn wǒ kāishǐ ...
Wǒmen liáotiān ba!	Wǒ gānggāng kāishǐ zuò ...
	Zì shàng cì wǒmen liáotiān ...
Conversation extensions	**Conversation details**
Nǐ xǐhuan ma? Nǐ jué de zěnmeyàng?	Zài jiā (where?) ... Shàng ge xīngqī (when?)
Hěn yǒuyìsi! Jìxù ba!	Wǒ chī guo ... Běijīng kǎoyā (what?)
	Xiànzài (when?) ... jiàozi (what?)

1 In Conversation 1, Lucy describes her hobby, cooking, then elaborates by adding descriptive details. Look back at the conversation to identify the details Lucy gives.

   a (when?) **Shàng yícì** (what?) _____

   b (what?) **Wǒ zuò** (how many times?) _____

   c (when?) **Xiànzài** (what?) _____

2 Can you find the other conversation components in Conversation 1? Highlight:

a two conversational warmers　　**b** two conversation starters

c two conversational leads　　　**d** one conversation extension

3 Now create some conversation starters using the verbs **zhīdao, kànjiàn** and **rènshi** (to know, be familiar with a person/thing).

a I know that you're English.

_____

_____

b Do you know Sarah's new friend? (hint: use **rènshi**)

_____

_____

c Have you already seen this movie?

_____

_____

PUT IT TOGETHER

1 What is your hobby? Pick a hobby you'd like to be able to describe. Use the phrases **Wǒ gānggāng kāishǐ** or **Wǒ zhèngzài …** along with vocab you look up to create two of your own conversation leads.

_____

_____

2 Now create a script in which you describe your hobby to a friend. Start with a conversational lead, but then go on to add details like:

⋯⋗ why/when you started it

⋯⋗ details of what you did last time

⋯⋗ what you've learned or achieved so far.

CONVERSATION 2

Your daily routine

What do you normally do in a day? In a week?

🔊 **08.03** Lucy and Wǎntíng are talking about their daily routines. How does Lucy say 'it was strange'? What helped her get into the swing of things?

This very Chinese word, which roughly translates as 'to take a stroll' perfectly describes going on a leisurely walk and is a common activity in the morning or after meals.

VOCABULARY: work
In Chinese, 'work' is **gōngzuò** – both the place and the action. If you're going to work, however, you can use **qù gōngzuò**, but you'll more often hear **shàngbān**. To leave work, you can use **xiàbān**.

Wǎntíng : Zài wǒ kànlái, duì nǐ láishuō zài Běijīng yíqiè dōu hěn hǎo.

Lucy : Duì. Wǒ yě zhème rènwéi. Qǐchū, yǒudiǎn qíguài, dànshì xiànzài xíguàn le. Měitiān zǎoshang **shàngbān** qián, wǒ chūqù zài wǒ jiā fùjìn **sànbù**.

Wǎntíng : Wǒ yěshì. Měi tiān xiàwǔ dài wǒ de gǒu qù Hòuhǎi sànbù. Yǒushí qí zìxíngchē.

Lucy : Wǒ dàochù qí zìxíngchē! Wǒ bú zuò dìtiě – wǒ xūyào xīnxiān kōngqì.

Wǎntíng : Wǒ yě bú zuò dìtiě. Wǒ chángcháng kāichē qù shàngbān.

Lucy : Xiàwǔ zài yí ge fēicháng hǎo de fànguǎn chī wǔfàn – zhèlǐ yǒu zuì hǎochī de huǒguō.

Wǎntíng : Dà duōshù shíhou, wǒ zài jiā zuòfàn, dànshì yǒushí chūqù chī. Zhè shì wǒ dìyī cì lái zhèlǐ.

Lucy : Nǐ cónglái méi lái guo wǒ zuì xǐhuan de fànguǎn ma? Nǐ yídìng yào lái chángchang! Wǒ qǐng nǐ!

FIGURE IT OUT

1 Who does what? Tick the correct box.

	goes for a walk before work	rides a bike	takes the car	always has lunch at a restaurant	sometimes tries new restaurants	prepares lunch at home
Lucy						
Wǎntíng						

2 Which phrase does Wǎntíng use to mean 'it seems to me' in the first line of the dialogue? Write it out here in Chinese. How is it used in the conversation: as a starter, warmer or extension?

_____   _____

_____   _____

3 Answer the questions in Chinese.

   a Shàngbān qián, Lucy zuò shénme?

   _____

   _____

   b Wǎntíng shénme shíhou dài tā de gǒu qù Hòuhǎi sànbù?

   _____

   _____

   c Lucy zài nǎli qí zìxíngchē?

   _____

   _____

   d Lucy wèishénme bú zuò dìtiě?

   _____

   _____

   e Wǎntíng zěnme qù gōngzuò?

   _____

   _____

NOTICE

🔊 **08.04** Listen to the audio and study the table.

Essential phrases for Conversation 2

Chinese	Meaning	Literal translation
... duì nǐ zài Běijīng yìqiè dōu hěn hǎo!	... Beijing has been good to you!	... against you located Beijing everything all very good!
Wǒ yě zhème rènwéi.	I also think so.	I also that way think.
Qǐchū, yǒudiǎn qíguài.	In the beginning, it's a little strange.	In the beginning, a little strange.
xíguàn le	used to it	habit [change marker]
zài ... fùjìn	near to ...	from ... near
sànbù	stroll	stroll
Yǒushí qí zixíngchē.	Sometimes I ride my bike.	Sometimes ride bike.
zuò dìtiě	take the subway	sit subway
xīnxiān kōngqì	fresh air	fresh air
kāichē	drive	drive car
dà duōshù shíhou	most of the time	big most time
Wǒ qǐng nǐ!	My treat!	I invite you!

1 This could be used as a conversation starter. Rephrase the statement (**zài wǒ kànlái**) **duì nǐ láishuō zài Běijīng yìqiè dōu hěn hǎo!** into a question. Hint, using 'isn't that right?' makes turning this into a question a cinch.

_____

_____

2 Use the conversation in this unit and previous units to fill in the table with 'detail phrases' you could use to answer the questions: When? How often? Why? How? Where? Some of these may be new to you, so don't be afraid to look them up in your Chinese/English dictionary.

Conversation details

Time		Manner	Place
When?	**How often?**	**Why? / How?**	**Where?**
morning **a**	often **e**	by car **k**	in the park **m**
afternoon **b**	sometimes **f**	by subway **l**	everywhere **n**
lunchtime/noon **c**	now and then **g**		to work **o**
before work **d**	rarely (very little) **h**		in the restaurant **p**
	always **i**		at home **q**
	never **j**		

PUT IT TOGETHER

Write a script describing different parts of your normal routine, hobbies or interests, and make sure to add detail phrases. You might talk about:

⋯⋗ how you get to work/school every day
⋯⋗ your hobbies, interests or other activities
⋯⋗ details of how often, when, where, why or how you do different things.

#LANGUAGEHACK: the rephrasing technique for talking your way through complicated sentences

When you speak in your native language, you're used to expressing yourself with a lot of complexity and nuance. So how do you convey your more complex thoughts and feelings when you are still only working with the very basics of the language?

Expressing yourself with even limited language skills is largely a matter of skilful rephrasing. You'll need to simplify your sentences to use words and phrases you are more comfortable with. Here's how to break it down.

Figure out the core idea

First, recognize that the rules of expressing yourself as an eloquent native do not (usually) apply to you as a beginner Chinese learner. The nuanced language you search for in your head, the desire to know how to say what you want, and how to convey the right tone and courtesy ... sometimes you have to just let all that go!

'I'm sorry ... I just overheard you speak Mandarin ... do you mind if I practice a few phrases with you? ... I hope I'm not bothering you ...'

Next, figure out the one core idea you're most trying to express, then simplify it dramatically. So the initial idea may become: 'You speak Mandarin? Me too! Let's chat.'

Finally, translate this simpler concept of 'piggy-backing' your idea off another expression that works just as well: **Nǐ huì shuō Zhōngwén ma? Wǒ yě shuō! Wǒmen liáotiān ba!**

Divide and conquer

Sometimes you'll find that one way to express yourself involves a long sentence with many commas, verb forms and other issues to solve. When this happens, you can take a 'divide and conquer' approach to split the sentence up.

Example: Tā xiànzài zhù zài Běijīng, zài nàli tā yùjiàn le tā de qīzi. Tā de qīzi de míngzi shì Anna. (He now lives in Beijing where he met his wife. Her name is Anna.)

➤ Tā xiànzài zhù zài Běijīng. Zài nàli tā yùjiàn le Anna. Anna shì tā de qīzi. (He now lives in Beijing. He met Anna there. Anna is his wife.)

The easiest way to split up a long sentence is to use reference words to break an idea into small sentences, but to make it clear that they expand on the same idea. You can also present them as a sequence of events. Don't be afraid to repeat keywords (like Anna) if you can't find easier references.

Let's consider another tricky sentence structure: **Wǒ jué de kàn Zhōngwén diànyǐng hěn yǒu yìsi.**

When you come across complicated sentences, you can use: **Wǒ yīnggāi kàn Zhōngwén diànyǐng. Hěn yǒu yìsi.**

YOUR TURN: use the Hack

1 Rephrase each of the lines given, with a shorter translation in Chinese that conveys a similar meaning, but avoids complicated grammar. ←

Remember, this is a skill, which means that practice is the key to getting better.

   a I'm so happy that we were able to come to the restaurant together.

   _____

   _____

   b I would really love it if you were willing to visit the Forbidden City with me.

   _____

   _____

   c I'd rather that we went to the supermarket later in the afternoon.

   _____

   _____

2 In each of these sentences, the original English uses forms you haven't learned yet in Chinese. A simpler Chinese version has been started for you – fill in the gaps to complete the simpler phrases.

   a Tā shuō Zhōngwén _____ de hěn hǎo, suǒyǐ tā qù

   _____ gōngzuò. Tā de xīn gōngzuò _____

   _____ _____. (Because he speaks Chinese very well, he got a new job in China that's very interesting.)

   b _____ wán le yǐhòu, tā qù le Xībānyá.

   _____ Xībānyá, tā _____ xué Xībānyá yǔ.

   (After completing his studies he traveled to Spain, where he began to learn Spanish.)

PUT IT TOGETHER

1 A Chinese friend has come to visit you in your hometown. Give your
local know-how for what your friend should do to get the best out of
the visit. Describe:

⋯⋗ the first thing that he/she could or would do
⋯⋗ the places you would visit and why
⋯⋗ the activities you would do together
⋯⋗ other insider tips.

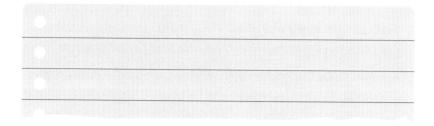

2 Now imagine that someone has invited you to go on an exotic
adventure – think kayaking down the Amazon River or climbing Mount
Everest. You'd have a lot of questions! Create a script that uses phrases
and questions to discuss an invitation like this in Mandarin. Use your
dictionary as often as you need. Be sure to:

⋯⋗ say when you'd have free time and when you could go
⋯⋗ ask for details of the trip – where it is, when it starts, when it ends
⋯⋗ ask about things you should bring
⋯⋗ talk about how you think it would be.

COMPLETING UNIT 8

Check your understanding

1 🔊 **08.05** Listen to the audio rehearsal in which a Mandarin speaker,
Liúwěi, describes his routine as well as things he wishes he could do.
Feel free to take notes or listen to it again.

2 🔊 **08.06** Now listen to questions about what you've just heard and
answer them out loud in Mandarin.

Show what you know...

Here's what you've just learned. Write or say an example for each item in the list. Then check off the ones you know.

- ☐ Write a short phrase that describes one of your hobbies.
- ☐ Give three different details about your hobby.
- ☐ Use **zuò** to talk about two different activities.
- ☐ Give three phrases that describe your normal routine using 'often', 'usually', 'sometimes', 'now and then', 'always' and 'never'.

MORE CHINESE CHARACTERS

In this unit, you'll learn more common radicals.

木 mù

The character for 'tree' is 木 and on its own as a character it is pronounced **mù**. It has four strokes, and as a radical, you'll see it in words like 林 (forest), 架 (shelf) and 树 (tree). The strokes are drawn in the following order:

Practice writing this character in the space below.

心 xīn

The Chinese character for 'heart' is used in words like 想 (want/would like) or 忘 (to forget).

It has four strokes. They are written in this order:

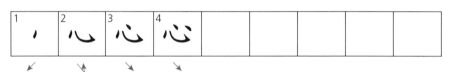

心 xīn
4 (strokes)

Practice writing this character in the space below.

力 lì

This character means 'strength' and it has just two strokes. It's used in characters like 助 (help) and 加 (to add).

Its strokes are written in this order:

力 lì
(2 strokes)

Practice writing this character in the space below.

车 chē

The final character in this unit is the character for 'car' in Chinese. You'll see it used both for the word 'car' and as a radical component in the characters for many different vehicles.

The character for 'car' is written in four strokes. As a radical, it's written as 车. You'll see it in characters like 轨 (rail) and 军 (military).

In character form, the strokes are drawn in this order:

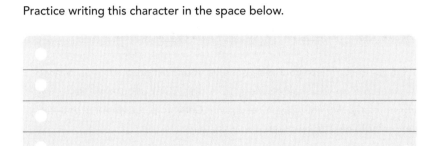

Practice writing this character in the space below.

COMPLETE YOUR MISSION

It's time to complete your mission: give your best productivity advice to be featured on your friend's vlog. To do this, think about the things you do regularly. You could even read some Chinese blogs about productivity and mindfulness to help you.

Try searching online for **shíjiān guǎnlǐ** (时间管理).

To complete this mission, go online to the #LanguageHacking community for help!

STEP 1: build your script

Keep building your script by using the phrases you've learned in this unit combined with 'me-specific' vocabulary to answer common questions about yourself. Be sure to:

⋯⟫ talk about different parts of your life and weekly routine
⋯⟫ describe where you go, how you get there and what you do
⋯⟫ include details of how often, when, where, why or how
⋯⟫ describe something else you would love to do but haven't done yet
⋯⟫ describe what you like about your routines and what could be better.
⋯⟫ write down your script, then repeat it until you feel confident.

When learning a new language, mistakes are inevitable. Part of the charm of speaking a second language is realizing that people are much less critical than you imagine!

STEP 2: learn from your mistakes, and others' ... online

The key is that if you're making mistakes, you're learning. And if you speak, you can even notice them better and fix them yourself. Added bonus: you can learn from the mistakes of other language hackers, too. So look at the corrections and comments people leave – you'll find that your common mistakes are most likely shared.

It's time to complete your mission. Share your productivity advice with the rest of the community! And in return, enjoy some free advice about how you can be more effective in your life. Go online and find your mission for Unit 8.

Use the community space to find out perhaps how you can make learning Chinese part of your daily routine.

STEP 3: learn from other learners

What productivity tips can you gain from other language hackers? After you've uploaded your own clip, check out what the other people in the community have to say about their routines. Your task is to tell at least three different people what was most useful about their routine.

This time, incorporate conversation starters, leads or extensions to help you get the conversation flowing, e.g. **Kàn qǐlái nǐ ...** (It seems that you ...).

STEP 4: reflect on what you learned

HEY, LANGUAGE HACKER, YOU'RE ALMOST THERE!

In this unit we talked a lot about the strategy behind preparing for the kinds of conversations you are likely to have. All the scripts you've been building are preparing you for this ultimate goal.

With the strategies you'll learn next in Missions 9 and 10, you will be amazed at how well your first conversation goes ...

Bú yào fàngqì!

NOTES

9 DESCRIBE IT!

Mission

Imagine this – you're applying to be a tour guide in a Mandarin-speaking city. You have to prove your ability to describe a place in detail and give recommendations for where to hang out and what to do.

Your mission is to pass for someone who has lived there for years by describing a city you know well (or want to know well!). Be prepared to do your research and give a short description of the highlights of what to do and see. But here's the twist – don't say the name of the city. See if others can guess! Describe the best places, explain their characteristics, and say how it might suit different personalities.

This mission will enable you to communicate more creatively by explaining the characteristics of people, places and things in the world around you in more detail.

Mission Prep:

⋯⋗ Describe places, landscapes and where you live: **sēnlín**, **shān**, **shùmù**, **hú**.

⋯⋗ Say what you miss using the verb **xiǎng**.

⋯⋗ Describe the weather and environment: **tiānqì hěn ...**

⋯⋗ Describe people and their personalities: **yǒnggǎn**, **gāo**, **ǎi**, **yǒuqù**

⋯⋗ Learn phrases for shopping: **mǎi**.

BUILDING LANGUAGE FOR DESCRIBING THE WORLD AROUND YOU!

You're getting closer to your first conversation with a native in Mandarin! You know how to say who the important people are in your life and what they do, but now you'll describe their personalities and characteristics as well. With this new vocab, you can express your thoughts more creatively in Mandarin – when you can't think of a word you need, just describe it instead!

#LANGUAGEHACK:
use your hidden moments to get Chinese immersion for the long-term

CONVERSATION 1

Describing the city

When you start talking to people from other countries, they are going to show interest in where you're from and how it's different from where they're from. Let's prepare you for these conversation topics now by building your script to describe different places.

🔊 **09.01** Lucy is getting ready to fly back to the US, and she's thinking about what she misses about home. She describes her hometown to her friend Xiǎowēi as they hang out on a sunny day. What does Lucy say to mean she's flying back to the US?

Lucy : Wǒ hěn kuài jiùyào huí Zhījiāgē le. Zhè shì wǒ zài Běijīng de zuìhòu yí ge xīngqī le.

Xiǎowēi : Tài zāogāo le! Xiǎng jiā ma?

Lucy : Wǒ xǐhuan Běijīng, dànshì wǒ zhù zài Zhījiāgē de jiāoqū, nǐ zhī bu zhīdao? Wǒ xiǎng nǎli de fēnwéi. Dànshì zhù zài Běijīng duì wǒ láishuō yě shì yìzhǒng xiǎngshòu. Dàjiā dōu fēicháng yǒuhǎo.

Xiǎowēi : Wǒ zhīdao. Wǒ yě huì xiǎng nǐ de! En, wǒ yǒu yí ge zhúyi … Nǐ yīnggāi mǎi yìxiē lǐwù sòng gěi nǐ de jiārén. Nàxiē lǐwù hái huì ràng nǐ xiǎngqǐ nǐ zài Běijīng de rìzi.

Lucy : Hǎo zhúyi! Wǒ ài gòuwù. Wǒ yīnggāi qù nǎli gòuwù?

Xiǎowēi : En … Nà yào kàn. Nǐ qù guo Nánluógǔxiàng ma? Zhè shì yí ge yǒumíng de hútòng. Hěn yǒu lìshǐ xìng, yě fēicháng piàoliang.

Lucy : Wǒ bù zhīdao … Yuǎn ma? Wǒ xiǎng sànbù.

Xiǎowēi : Yǒu diǎn yuǎn. Tā lí Hòuhǎi hěn jìn. Gòuwù yǐhòu, wǒmen kěyǐ qù Hòuhǎi sànbù.

Lucy : Ránhòu wǒmen lèi le, kěyǐ zhǎo ge dìfang chī bīngqílín.

Xiǎowēi : Nà tài wánměi le! Wǒmen zǒu ba!

FIGURE IT OUT

←

1 The following sentences are **cuò**. Highlight the word(s) that make them incorrect and write the Chinese words that are **duì**.

a **Zhè shì Lucy zài Běijīng de zuìhòu yì tiān.** (It's Lucy's last day in Beijing.)

_____

_____

b **Lucy yīnggāi mǎi yìxiē shū sòng gěi tā de jiārén.** (Lucy should buy some books to give her family.)

_____

_____

c **Shànghǎi shì yí ge yǒumíng de hútòng.** (Shanghai is a very famous hutong.)

_____

_____

d **Gòuwù qián, tāmen qù Hòuhǎi sànbù.** (Before shopping, they're taking a walk around Houhai.)

_____

_____

2 Use your understanding of the conversation to figure out the meaning of the phrases.

a Lucy shares how much time she has left in Beijing. What is the meaning of: **Zuìhòu yí ge xīngqī?**

_____

_____

b Xiǎowēi is saddened to hear Lucy is leaving Beijing. What do you think she means when she says: **Tài zāogāo le?**

_____

_____

c After they get tired, they plan to have an ice cream. What do you think Lucy suggests when she says: **Ránhòu...** ?

_____

_____

3 Answer the questions in Chinese.

a **Lucy shénme shíhou fēi huí Zhījiāgē?**

_____

_____

By now you have a great base of Chinese vocabulary, so now it's even more important for you to actively fill in your gaps. It's a good idea to highlight any new words you come across and make a note to add them to your script or study materials.

b Lucy xiǎng jiāoqū de shénme?

_____

_____

c Lucy jué de Xiǎowēi de zhúyi zěnmeyàng?

_____

_____

d Lucy yào mǎi shénme?

_____

_____

e Lucy xiǎng qù hútòng ma? Wèishénme?

_____

_____

f Lucy hé Xiǎowēi lèi le de shíhou, tāmen xiǎng zuò shénme?

_____

_____

4 Using context along with words you already know, find the Chinese phrases in the conversation for the bold text below and write them out.

a Xiǎowēi asks Lucy, '**Do you miss your family?**'

_____

_____

b At home, Lucy **lives in the suburbs.**

_____

_____

c In Beijing, Lucy thinks everyone is **extremely friendly.**

_____

_____

d How does Lucy say, '**I love shopping**'?

_____

_____

e When Lucy asks where she should go shopping, Xiǎowēi replies, 'Uh… **That depends.**'

_____

_____

NOTICE

🔊 **09.02** Listen to the audio and study the table.

Essential phrases for Conversation 1

Chinese	Meaning	Literal translation
hěn kuài jiùyào huí	go back very soon	very only want fast return
zuìhòu yí ge xīngqī	final week	last one week
Tài zāogāo le!	That's too bad!	Too bad [change marker]!
zhù zài jiāoqū	live in the suburbs	live located suburbs
fēnwéi	ambience	ambience
yìzhǒng xiǎngshòu	a kind of enjoyment	a type enjoyment
Dàjiā dōu fēicháng yǒuhǎo.	Everyone is extremely friendly.	Everyone extremely friendly.
mǎi yìxiē lǐwù sòng gěi nǐ de jiārén	buy some gifts to give your ambience	buy some gift give give you of ambience
huì ràng nǐ xiǎngqǐ nǐ zài Běijīng de rìzi	can remind you of your time in Beijing	is able bring memory you located Beijing of time
Wǒ ài gòuwù.	I love shopping.	I love shopping.
Nà yào kàn.	It depends.	That want look.
yí ge yǒumíng de hútòng	a famous hútòng	one [measure word] famous of hútòng
Hěn yǒu lìshǐ xìng, yě fēicháng piàoliang.	It's very historical, also extremely pretty.	Very historical, also extremely pretty.
Yuǎn ma?	Is it far?	Far [question marker]?
lí … hěn jìn	from … very close	from … very close
kěyǐ zhǎo ge dìfang chī bīngqílín	we can find somewhere to eat ice cream	can find [measure word] place eat ice cream
Nà tài wánměi le!	That's perfect!	That extremely perfect [change marker]!
Wǒmen zǒu ba!	Let's go!	We go [suggestion marker]!

1 For each item below, find the first phrase in the phrase list, then write it out in Chinese. Next, use this to translate the second phrase that follows.

a Do you miss your family?

_____

_____

I'll miss you, too.

_____

_____

b I'm going back

_____

_____

I'm going back soon.

_____

_____

c I enjoy

_____

_____

I truly enjoy living in Beijing.

_____

_____

d When we're tired ...

_____

_____

When we're tired we can relax (**xiūxí**).

_____

_____

2 Match the Chinese phrases with their correct English translations.

a **Nà yào kàn!**   1 It depends!

b **Wǒmen zǒu ba!**   2 Good idea!

c **Tài zāogāo le!**   3 That's too bad!

d **Hǎo zhúyi!**   4 Let's go!

3 A good memory technique is to learn vocab in 'clusters' – learning words of a similar theme together. Use your dictionary to fill in the lettered blanks in the vocab tables.

Landscape and nature vocab

Chinese	Meaning	Chinese	Meaning
a	countryside	sēnlín	forest
shān	**b**	shùmù	**c**
hú	lake	**d**	sun

City vocabulary

Chinese	Meaning	Chinese	Meaning
e	bank	**f**	police station
diàn	shop	**g**	city hall
yàodiàn	**h**	**i**	stadium
miànbāo diàn	bakery	bǎihuò shāngdiàn	department store
jiē	street	gōngyuán	park
bówùguǎn	museum	**j**	library

PRACTICE

1 Look up new words you'd need to describe where you live and the landscape in your area. Do you live near the ocean? In the suburbs? In a third-story walk-up? Add your 'me-specific' vocab to the landscape and nature vocab list.

2 Use the vocab you've just looked up to practice describing where you live.

Example: I live in ... Around the corner, there is / there are …

_____

_____

3 Now do the same about a family member or friend.

Example: He / she lives near … On his / her street, there is / there are …

_____

_____

VOCAB EXPLANATION: talking about the weather

Tiānqì zěnmeyàng? – What's the weather like? (lit. 'Weather how about?').
When you want to describe the weather, you'll use the word for weather:
tiānqì. Most of the time, you'll simply need to say **Tiānqì** + description.

Tiānqì … hǎo (nice) / **bù hǎo** (bad) / **rè** (hot) / **lěng** (cold) / **liángkuài** (cool)
/ **wēnnuǎn** (warm) / **cháoshī** (humid)

There are a few exceptions where different structures are used:

Xiàyǔ le (it's raining)

Worried about remembering the structures for these exceptions? It's best to learn them as language chunks because they are useful Chinese phrases you can use to discuss the weather.

1 Practice creating new sentences in Chinese to describe the weather.

   a It's nice out.

   _____

   _____

   b The weather is bad. What a pity!

   _____

   _____

2 Use **tiānqì** to make two sentences describing the weather where you
are right now.

   _____

   _____

PUT IT TOGETHER

You now have a greater ability to talk about your environment, so let's put that into action!

Create a script in which you describe where you live or a place that you
love to visit, in as much detail as possible. Be sure to include descriptive
words (adjectives and pronouns) and answer the questions:

⋯⋗ What is the landscape like?
⋯⋗ What is the weather usually like? Sometimes like?
⋯⋗ What would you miss most about it?

GRAMMAR EXPLANATION: separable verbs

Chinese has a type of verb known as a separable verb. These are verbs that can be separated in certain contexts as you saw with **zhī bu zhīdao**. Separable verbs can be identified because the first part of the word is the verb while the second part of the word is the object.

Other separable verbs are **shuìjiào** (to sleep) / **jiànmiàn** (to meet) / **yóuyǒng** (to swim) / etc.

When duplicating the verb to soften its meaning or add emphasis, you double the verb as in **jiànjian miàn** (it's not **jiànmiàn jianmiàn**).

1 Put the following separable verbs into the past tense using **guò**:

   a chīfàn (eat a meal) _____

   b shuìjiào (sleep) _____

   c kāihuì (hold a meeting) _____

2 Duplicate the following verbs to soften their meaning:

   a páiduì (line up) _____

   b qǐngjià (ask for vacation time) _____

   c pǎobù (run) _____

3 Use the following verbs to form a yes or no question:

   a kànbìng (go to the doctor) _____

   b liáotiān (chat) _____

   c chūchāi (go on a business trip) _____

CONVERSATION 2

Describing personalities

Now let's focus on a whole new set of descriptive words you can use to talk about people and their personalities.

🔊 09.03 Lucy and Xiǎowēi are now shopping and discuss what gifts Lucy should get for her family, based on their personalities. What words does Lucy use to describe her sister, brother and parents?

VOCABULARY: 'we'
Chinese has two different words that mean 'we' – **zánmen** and **wǒmen**. How do you know which to use? **Zánmen** is used when the listener is included. **Wǒmen** is used when the listener is not necessarily included.

For example:

Zánmen qù kàn diànyǐng ba! – (Let's go see a movie!) (You and I)

Wǒmen kàn le yí ge diànyǐng. – (We saw a movie.) (Implying that you and someone other than the listener saw a movie together. The person you are talking with may not be included.)

Lucy : Zhè tiáo hútòng tài bàng le! Yǒu hěn duō dōngxi yào kàn!

Xiǎowēi : Nǐ zhīdao yào mǎi shénme ma?

Lucy : Wǒ xiǎng wèi zìjǐ mǎi hěn duō dōngxi. Dànshì bù zhīdao wèi jiārén mǎi shénme.

Xiǎowēi : Gēn wǒ shuōshuo nǐ de jiārén ba.

Lucy : Nà hěn nán … bǐrú shuō, wǒ de mèimèi hěn yǒnggǎn. Yǒu yìtiān, tā zhēn xiǎng yí ge rén lái Běijīng. Wǒ yīnggāi gěi tā mǎi jìniànpǐn ma?

Xiǎowēi : Nǐ kěyǐ gěi tā mǎi chá, duì bu duì? Hái yǒu yìxiē tángguǒ. Hái yào gěi **zánmen** zìjǐ mǎi yìxiē tángguǒ!

Lucy : Míngbai le! Wǒ de dìdi ne? Tā hěn niánqīng. Tā kěnéng huì rènwéi jìniànpǐn hěn wúliáo. Tā zhǐ xǐhuan diànzǐ yóuxì. Wǒ yīnggāi mǎi shénme?

Xiǎowēi : Diànzǐ yóuxì pèijiàn zěnmeyàng? Diànzǐ chǎnpǐn zài Zhōngguó fēicháng piányi. Nǐ zhīdao ma?

Lucy : A, duì. Zhè ràng wǒ xiǎng qǐ lái … tā de ěrjī huài le. Wǒ de fùmǔ xǐhuan chuántǒng de dōngxi. Wǒ kěyǐ gěi tāmen mǎi yí tào chájù.

Xiǎowēi : Hǎo zhúyì! Kěnéng nǐ yě kěyǐ mǎi yì xiē chábēi.

FIGURE IT OUT

1 **Duì háishì cuò?** Select the correct answer.

   a Lucy is shopping for her friends.   **duì / cuò**

   b Xiǎowēi helps Lucy with ideas for presents.   **duì / cuò**

   c Lucy knows exactly what to buy.   **duì / cuò**

2 Read the questions. Then complete the answers in Chinese.

   a Lucy xiǎng gěi mèimèi mǎi shénme?

   _____ _____ hé

   _____ _____

   b Wèishénme? Lucy guānyú mèimèi shuō le shénme? Tā

   _____ _____

   c Lucy de dìdi yào bu yào diǎnxíng de jìniànpǐn? Tā rènwéi jìniànpǐn
   hěn _____ _____

   d Guānyú fùmǔ, Lucy shuō le shénme?

   Tāmen xǐhuan _____ _____.

3 Find the following phrases in the conversation and highlight them. Then write out the Chinese.

a that reminds me _____

b she truly wants _____

c a souvenir _____

d for myself _____

e traditional things _____

f very boring _____

CULTURE TIP: tea
Tea holds an important place in Chinese culture and when you walk around Beijing, you'll come across a wide variety of tea shops where you can buy tea, teapots, tea cups, and even teasets. In China, black tea is called **hóng chá** (literally: red tea).

NOTICE

🔊 **09.04** Listen to the audio and study the table.

Essential phrases for Conversation 2

Chinese	Meaning	Literal translation
Wǒ xiǎng wèi zìjǐ mǎi hěn duō dōngxi.	I would like to buy myself lots of things.	I would like for the sake of myself buy very many thing.
Gēn wǒ shuōshuo nǐ de jiārén ba.	Tell me about your family	With I speak speak you of family [suggestion marker].
Wǒ de mèimei hěn yǒnggǎn.	My younger sister is very brave.	I of younger sister very brave.
Wǒ yīnggāi gěi tā mǎi jìniànpǐn ma?	Should I buy her a souvenir?	I should give her buy souvenir [question marker]?
Hái yǒu yìxiē tángguǒ.	There's also candy.	Still have some candy.
Tā kěnéng huì rènwéi jìniànpǐn hěn wúliáo.	He might think a souvenir is boring.	He maybe able think souvenir very boring.
Diànzǐ yóuxì pèijiàn zěnmeyàng?	How about video game accessories?	Video game accessory how about?
Diànzǐ chǎnpǐn zài Zhōngguó fēicháng piányi.	Electronic products are extremely cheap in China.	Electronic product located China extremely cheap.
Zhè ràng wǒ xiǎng qǐ lái …	That reminds me …	This make I think rise come …
tā de ěrjī huài le	his headphones are broken	he of headphone broke [change marker]
Wǒ de fùmǔ xǐhuan chuántǒng de dōngxi.	My parents like traditional things.	I of parents like traditional of thing.

1 Find six adjectives in the conversation and write them here.

a _____

b _____

c _____

d _____

e _____

f _____

2 Another effective memory technique is to learn new words in pairs with their opposites. Use the adjectives from the phrase list and a dictionary to complete the sentences.

a **Zhè bú tài** _____ **zhè hěn** _____
   (It's not too easy, it's hard.)

b **Zhè bú** _____ **zhè hěn** _____
   (It's not unique, it's typical.)

c **Nà bú** _____, **nà hěn** _____
   (That isn't stupid, that is intelligent.)

d **Tāmen bú** _____, **tāmen hěn** _____
   (They aren't modern, they are traditional.)

e **Tā bù** _____, **tā hěn** _____
   (She's not brave, she's shy.)

f **Tā bù** _____, **tā hěn** _____
   (He's not old, he's young.)

GRAMMAR TIP:
adjectives in Chinese
In Chinese, the grammar tied to adjectives functions differently than in English. You may have noticed that **de** goes between the adjective and the noun. This is generally the case when the adjective has more than one syllable. If the adjective is only one syllable, the **de** may be dropped. For example:

là cài (spicy food) – one syllable

hóngsè de yǐzi (red chair) – two syllables

The exception is when you stack adjectives as in the example below (a single-syllable adjective paired with another adjective gets **de**):

fēicháng dà de chē (extremely big car)

3 Complete the table with the missing adjectives based off the corresponding translation. Use your dictionary to look them up if you need to.

Chinese	Meaning	Chinese	Meaning
a	shy/timid	yǒnggǎn	**b**
c	ugly	**d**	beautiful/pretty
gāo	**e**	ǎi	short (refers to height)
yǒuqù	**f**	**g**	typical
h	unpleasant	yǒu tóngqíng xīn	nice
bēiguān	**i**	**j**	optimistic
k	proud	qiānxū	**l**
m	funny	rènzhēn	**n**
bèn	**o**	cōngmíng	**p**
àomàn	arrogant	**q**	wise/smart
pǔtōng	**r**	**s**	friendly

4 Create new sentences with adjectives that describe things in your life. Be sure to look up words in your dictionary if you need to!

a Wǒ hěn _____ _____

  Wǒ de gōngzuò hěn _____ _____

b Wǒ de fùqīn / péngyou / dìdi hěn _____

  _____

  Tā de fángzi hěn _____ _____

c Wǒ de mǔqīn / jiějie / nǚpéngyou hěn _____

  _____

PUT IT TOGETHER

Prepare for these questions now by creating a script in which you explain the personalities of at least two important people in your life. Make your script as 'me-specific' as possible by looking up any new descriptive words you'll need now, so you'll have them ready during your conversations.

⋯⟩ Describe two different people in your life.
⋯⟩ Use adjectives to describe their personalities.
⋯⟩ Include sentences that use different word orders.

Use the conversation strategy to avoid adjectives when possible (but don't worry about adjective endings when you can't avoid them).

Example: Wǒ jiějie hěn yǒuqù / wǒ yǒuqù de jiějie

GRAMMAR EXPLANATION: the big one

Whenever you want to say things like 'the big one', 'the blue one' or 'the small ones', you can drop the noun and maintain the adjective + **de** structure. For example, let's say you're choosing between a red and a blue shirt. In Chinese, this would be the **hóngsè de chènshān** (red shirt) versus the **lánsè de chènshān** (blue shirt). If you would like to say 'the red one', you drop the noun (shirt) and say **hóngsè de**. If you want to say 'the blue one', you say **lánsè de**.

1 If you needed to describe an item you wanted to a shopkeeper, you could use the following phrases from this conversation. Write them out in Chinese.

   a the serious one _____ _____

   b the red one _____ _____

   c the green one _____ _____

   d the best one _____ _____

2 Practice creating new questions in Chinese that you could use to ask about things when shopping.

   a How much does the black one cost?

   _____

   _____

   b Can I buy the green one now?

   _____

   _____

c Do you accept credit cards? (lit: credit card, is that okay?)

_____

_____

d A little cheaper. (lit: cheap a little)

_____

_____

3 Fill in the missing translations in the table.

Adjective	Meaning	Color	Meaning
cháng	**a**	huángsè	yellow
duǎn	short (refers to time)	hóngsè	red
kuān	wide	lánsè	blue
ǎi	**b**	báisè	white
àn	dark	lǜsè	green
hòu	thick	hēisè	black
shòu	**c**	huīsè	gray
		zōnghèsè	brown

PUT IT TOGETHER

Nǐ zài zhǎo shénme? (What are you looking for?)

Now it's time to build sentences you could use to describe something you are looking for, want to buy or have lost. Think of one or two items to describe, and then be as creative as you can to describe the item without using the word for the item itself. You might include:

⋯⋗ what it looks like, what you need it for or what type of person you're getting it for
⋯⋗ what brand it is or what color it is
⋯⋗ a description using 'this' or 'that one' or 'the ... one'
⋯⋗ any other descriptive adjectives that you know!

_____

_____

_____

_____

#LANGUAGEHACK: use your hidden moments to get Chinese immersion for the long-term

Rather than thinking about how many months or years it may take to learn Chinese, an incredibly effective learning strategy is to focus instead on the minutes it takes.

The minutes you put into your language every day are what truly count. Not everyone has a few hours every day to devote to Chinese – but everyone has a few minutes. Even if you live a busy lifestyle, you can still find 'hidden moments' throughout your day for Chinese practice.

Standing in line at the supermarket, waiting for the elevator, sitting in a bus, train or taxi, waiting for a tardy friend ... all of these are wasted moments in our days. These moments are perfect for squeezing Chinese practice into your daily life.

Instead of making a distinction between 'study blocks' of Chinese, why not blend it into your life to make language learning a habit?

Chinese immersion – from anywhere

As you've followed Lucy's story, perhaps you've thought how lucky she is to go to China to improve her Chinese through immersion! But in fact, thanks to technology, you can create a Chinese immersion environment from anywhere in the world, no matter where you live.

When you do have bigger windows of time to practice Chinese, you can create an at-home immersion environment in loads of different ways:

You can connect with other learners (like you've been doing with our online community!) to get practice with them through regular video/audio calls.

Don't overlook the value of these short periods of time. They really add up, and more importantly, they're a great way to consistently keep up momentum in your learning.

LEARNING STRATEGY:
study on the go
When I'm learning a new language, I always use a vocab study app and other tools designed for use on the go and pull them out whenever I'm waiting around. Since my smartphone is with me anyway, I use it to learn what I can, when I can, even if it's just a word or two. See our Resources for some suggestions!

You can listen to live streaming radio or watch streaming video from China (or another Mandarin-speaking country) online.

Do you play **diànzǐ yóuxì**? You can change the language settings on your games to Chinese!

You can also change the language of websites you use often and even your computer and smartphone operating system to Chinese.

You'll see it's not that bad, and you can always change it back if you find it too hard. Usually, you'll just need to look for (Yǔ) yán (语言) under 'Configuration'.

YOUR TURN: use the Hack

1 Look at the apps and online Resources we recommend. Pick a few to start with, then add them to your computer or smartphone now so they are ready and waiting for you during your hidden moments.

2 Look at the websites, apps, games, browsers and even the operating system you use the most, and see if they have an option to change the language to Chinese. Since you are already used to the interface and know where you'd normally click or tap, why not go ahead and change the language?

COMPLETING UNIT 9

Check your understanding

1 ◀) **09.05** Listen to this audio rehearsal, in which someone describes their environment and people around them. Feel free to take notes or listen to it multiple times.

2 ◀) **09.06** Next, listen to the questions about the audio rehearsal that you've just heard and answer the questions out loud in Mandarin.

Show what you know...

Here's what you've just learned. Write or say an example for each item in the list. Then check off the ones you know.

- ☐ Say something you miss using **xiǎng**.
- ☐ Give two sentences describing where you live.
- ☐ Say 'it's hot', 'it's cold' and 'it's humid'.
- ☐ Give a sentence that uses an adjective to describe a family member's personality. Put the adjective in the right position in the sentence.
- ☐ Use three different adjectives to describe your favorite clothes in Chinese. Put the adjectives in the right word order and gender.
- ☐ Ask the questions, 'Can I pay with a credit card?' and 'Can you make it cheaper?'.

MORE CHINESE CHARACTERS

In this unit, you'll learn six of the most common Chinese characters you'll come across. You've already learned several common characters in past units like: 一, 不, 人, 我 and 他, among others. So let's look at six more common characters you haven't yet learned.

了 le

The character for the change marker you've used often in these last several lessons is 了. It has two strokes and they are drawn in the following order:

了 **le; liǎo**
(2 strokes)

1 ↗	2 了								

Practice writing this character in the space below.

是 shì

The Chinese character for 'to be' 是 is used often, so it's an important character to recognize. The top half of the character has 日 (the sun). At the bottom, it includes the bottom half of 走 (to go, to walk). It suggests you are very certain about where you're going when the sun is out.

It has nine strokes. They are written in this order:

Practice writing this character in the space below.

在 zài

This character means 'located' and you've used it to talk about location (on earth). This is why the character 在 has 土 (earth) at the bottom. It has six strokes.

Its strokes are written in this order:

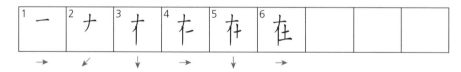

Practice writing this character in the space below.

有 yǒu

Another word you've come across often in the dialogues and exercises is 有 (to have). In this character, 月 represents a piece of bacon. The two lines at the top represent a hand holding the bacon with a rope. This comes from the idea that when you have bacon, you 'have' in comparison to those who 'have not'.

The character for 'to have' is written in six strokes and they are drawn in this order:

有 yǒu
(6 strokes)

Practice writing this character in the space below.

这 zhè

One of the final characters you'll learn in this unit is 这. This character means 'this' or 'here' in Chinese. It includes 辶, the walk radical, because you need to walk in order to come here. It has seven strokes drawn in this order:

这 zhè
(7 strokes)

Practice writing this character in the space below.

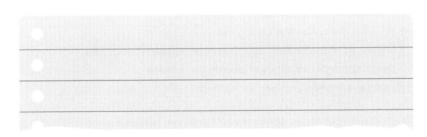

那 nà

The last character in this unit is the character for 'that' in Chinese. Pay special attention to the left part of the character. It is not 月. 'That' has six strokes drawn in this order:

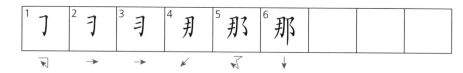

Practice writing this character in the space below.

COMPLETE YOUR MISSION

It's time to complete your mission: pass for a local and use your descriptive language to point out the best places in town to a foreigner. To do this, you'll need to describe the details and characteristics of different places, people and things.

STEP 1: build your script

Think about your favorite city. What does it look like? How would you describe the buildings, the atmosphere and the people? Build a script you can use to give more detailed descriptions of places, people and things.

⋯⟩ describe what it's like in your favorite city
⋯⟩ say what type of landscape is nearby
⋯⟩ say what the weather is usually like
⋯⟩ explain what the houses, apartments or neighborhoods look like
⋯⟩ describe the personalities of people living there
⋯⟩ incorporate new verbs you've learned

Write down your script, then repeat it until you feel confident.

STEP 2: a little goes a long way ... online

This is your last dress rehearsal before you speak one-on-one with a native speaker! If you're feeling good about your script, go ahead and give it another go! Go online, find your Unit 9 mission, and share your recording with the community for feedback and encouragement.

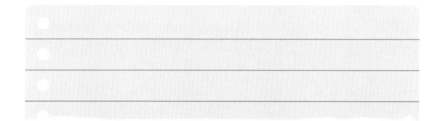

Learn every day, even if it's just a little. You will learn more if you distribute your practice.

STEP 3: learn from other learners

How did other language hackers describe their city? What city are they describing? Would you hire them as a tour guide? Ask them two more questions about the city.

STEP 4: reflect on what you learned

Did you learn any new words or phrases in the community space? Did you find a new place to add to your bucket list? What did you learn about the gaps in your scripts?

HEY, LANGUAGE HACKER, ARE YOU READY?!

You've just learned how to describe pretty much anything, as well as how to work around any gaps you may have in your Chinese. I know you're ready for the ultimate mission!

Jìxù ba!

NOTES

10 HAVING YOUR FIRST CONVERSATION

Mission

You've worked hard. You've kept at it. And now, you're armed with a solid base in the Chinese language. ←

Your mission is to have a one-on-one conversation – online with video activated – with a native Mandarin speaker.

This mission will set you up with the phrases, the confidence and an insider look at how to have your first conversation in Mandarin – even if you don't think you're ready.

More importantly, you know how to use clever #languagehacks and conversation strategies to make the Chinese phrases you know stretch even further for you.

Mission prep

⋯❯ Prepare the essential phrases you need to have a conversation.
⋯❯ Develop the mindset: overcome nerves and don't worry about the grammar.
⋯❯ Find a language partner and schedule your first conversation!
⋯❯ Apply what you've learned in the context of a first conversation.

BUILDING LANGUAGE FOR HAVING A CONVERSATION

Here's where all of the vocabulary – and just as importantly – all of the conversation strategies you've learned over the past nine units come into play. You're going to have your first 'face-to-face' conversation with another Mandarin speaker!

Face-to-face conversations with a native Mandarin speaker can be intimidating. That's why I like to 'cheat' by having my first few conversations in a new language with a partner online. This takes off the pressure, and you have the added luxury of being able to quickly search for words or phrases with online translators and dictionaries. Let's take a look at how you can strategize your own first conversations!

#LANGUAGEHACK:
develop a cheat sheet and go into 'autopilot' during your first conversation

YOUR FIRST CONVERSATION

🔊 **10.01** Listen to this 'first' conversation between a language hacker (LH) and his Mandarin conversation partner. It will give you a good idea of how a typical first conversation in Mandarin might start. As you listen, highlight any words or phrases you'd like to use in your own first conversation with a native speaker.

Yǔqǐ : Nǐ hǎo.

LH : Nǐ hǎo. Nǐ jiào shénme míngzi?

Yǔqǐ : Wǒ jiào Yǔqǐ. Nǐ ne?

LH : Wǒ jiào Benny.

Yǔqǐ : Hěn gāoxìng rènshi nǐ. Suǒyǐ gàosu wǒ ba, nǐ zhù zài nǎli?

LH : Wǒ shì Ài'ěrlán rén, dànshì wǒ zhù zài Niǔyuē.

Yǔqǐ : A, hěn yǒuyìsi. Ài'ěrlán. Wǒ cóng méi qù guo Ài'ěrlán, dànshì wǒ èrshí suì de shíhou qù guo Niǔyuē. Nǐ lái guo Zhōngguó ma?

LH : Hái méiyou. Wǒ xiǎng yǒu yìtiān néng qù Zhōngguó. Duìbùqǐ … Wǒ gānggāng kāishǐ xué Zhōngwén. Qǐng shuō màn yìdiǎn.

Yǔqǐ : Dāngrán kěyǐ!

LH : Nǐ hěn nàixīn! Xièxie nǐ. Nǐ jiāo Zhōngwén duōjiǔ le?

PUT YOUR CONVERSATION STRATEGIES INTO ACTION

What should I say?

Every conversation has a certain 'formula' – phrases you can expect the conversation to include. We've talked a lot about this throughout this book. You can use the expected nature of conversations to your advantage.

Imagine that you are talking with our native Mandarin speaker, Yǔqǐ, for your own first conversation in Mandarin. In this case, the conversation will flow in a slightly different way. Use the prompts given to practice applying phrases you know, and fill in the gaps in the conversation.

Yǔqǐ: Nǐ hǎo. Hěn gāoxìng rènshi nǐ.

LH: (Greet your language partner.)

1 _____ _____

Yǔqǐ: Wǒ jiào Yǔqǐ. Nǐ ne?

LH: (Give your name and tell Yǔqǐ that it's nice to meet her.)

2 _____ _____

Yǔqǐ: Nǐ wèishénme xué Zhōngwén?

LH: (Answer her question about why you're learning Chinese.)

3 _____ _____

Yǔqǐ: Nà hěn bàng! Nǐ huì shuō qítā yǔyán ma?

LH: (Share what other languages you speak.)

4 _____ _____

Yǔqǐ: Wǒ de Jiānádà xuésheng gàosu wǒ zhè mén yǔyán hěn nán!

LH: (Say that you couldn't understand what she said. Ask her to write it out.)

5 _____ _____

Yǔqǐ: Dāngrán. Wǒ yǒu yí ge Jiānádà xuésheng. Tā jué de zhè mén yǔyán hěn nán.

Now that you've seen two examples of a first conversation in action, let's start preparing you for the real thing.

#LANGUAGEHACK: develop a cheat sheet to go into 'autopilot' during your first conversation

Here's how I know you can handle this conversation, even if you think you're not ready: because you're going to 'cheat', so to speak.

There is no shame in 'cheating' here. This isn't an exam. This is a conversation. Consider your cheat sheet as a crutch that helps you make the transition from studying Chinese to speaking Mandarin. By using a cheat sheet now, you will get to the point where you don't need it a lot faster. It gives you momentum so that you become a lot more experienced at speaking over less time.

I like to prepare for my conversations online by making up a cheat sheet of words and phrases I plan to use during the conversation – and I can have it right in front of me (on paper, in another window or on another device) the whole time.

We'll do the same thing for you. You're going to have your own phrases ready, planned out and written out in front of you, so you'll be able to glance at them while you're speaking Mandarin. This way, it doesn't matter if your mind goes blank. You'll just take a breath and look at your cheat sheet.

Let's get to work preparing your cheat sheet. I like to separate mine into four parts:

1 Essential phrases

2 Survival phrases

3 Questions I plan to ask

4 'Me-specific' phrases

Essential phrases

My essential phrases are the words and phrases I know I'll need to use in every conversation. These are usually greetings and sign-off words, as well as questions I expect to be asked and my planned answers.

I've started you off with some suggestions. Write out the ones you plan to use in Chinese, and then add some new ones of your own.

Essential phrases

(refer to units 1–3 for inspiration.)

Greetings	Sign-offs
Nǐ hǎo! Nǐ zuìjìn zěnmeyàng?	Xiàcì jiàn!
Nǐ hǎo, hěn gāoxìng rènshi nǐ!	Wǒ xiān zǒu le.

(Refer to Units 1–6 for inspiration.)

Typical questions	Prepared answers
Nǐ jiào shénme míngzi?	
Nǐ shì nǐ guò rén?	
Nǐ zhù zài nǎli?	
Nǐ zuò shénme gōngzuò?	
Nǐ wèishénme xué Zhōngwén?	
Nǐ huì shuō qítā yǔyán ma?	

Don't worry about thinking up every possible word or phrase you might need. It's impossible and it's not a good use of your time! Instead, let the language tell you what you need to learn. Use the language you know now in natural conversation – however much or little it may be – and you'll quickly learn the 'me-specific' phrases that you haven't (yet!) added to your script.

Survival phrases

Don't be afraid of making mistakes in Chinese. Instead, expect them. Prepare for them. Have a plan for dealing with difficult moments. Even if you forget every word you know or can't understand a single word the other person is saying, you can still have a conversation if you've prepared your survival phrases.

In the heat of the moment there's a lot to think about. Don't worry about saying single words to get your point across. You can always add a **qǐng** to the beginning to make sure your partner knows you don't mean to be impolite!

Here are some suggestions. Add some new ones of your own.

Survival phrases
(Refer to Unit 3 for inspiration.)

Full phrases	Or shorten them!
Nǐ kěyǐ děng yíxià ma?	Děng yíxià.
Nǐ kěyǐ bǎ zhè ge xiě xiàlái ma?	Kěyǐ xiě xiàlái ma?
Qǐng nǐ zài shuō yíbiàn.	Zài shuō yíbiàn.
Nǐ kěyǐ shuō màn yìdiǎn ma?	Màn yìdiǎn
Wǒ bù míngbai.	Shénme?

Speaking Mandarin with a new person gives you an opportunity to learn about that person's life, language and culture! I make sure I prepare in advance if there's anything in particular I'm curious to know.

Questions I plan to ask

Plan out a few questions that you can ask the other person. You can use them to take the pressure off you, while the other person talks for a while. And they are great to have ready for when there's a lull in the conversation. You might ask about:

···⟩ life in the other person's country (**Zhōngguó rè ma?**)

···⟩ the Chinese language (**Zhè ge jùzi 'lìng yì fāngmiàn' – shì shénme yìsi?**)

···⟩ the other person's life work, or hobbies (**Zhōumò nǐ xǐhuan zuò shénme?**).

···⟩ I've already mentioned a few good options, but make sure you add some more of your own.

Prepared questions
(Refer to Units 2–9 for inspiration.)

... tiānqì zěnmeyàng?

Zhōngwén ... zěnme shuō?

_____ _____

_____ _____

_____ _____

'Me-specific' phrases I want to practice

These are the conversation topics specific to me that I want to practice – my interests, what I've been doing lately, what my upcoming plans are and the people in my life.

In your first conversation, if you've practiced your essential phrases and your survival phrases, everything else is just a bonus! I like to create a goal of a few new phrases I want to practice during each conversation. But keep it to just a few – between two and five phrases – which is plenty to accomplish in your first conversation. You could prepare to talk about:

···❯ what you're interested in (**Wǒ xǐhuan kēhuàn** [sci-fi]!)
···❯ what you've been doing today or lately (**Wǒ dú le yì piān Zhōngwén wénzhāng.**)
···❯ what your upcoming plans are (**Zhè zhōumò wǒ xiǎng chūqù tiàowǔ.**)
···❯ the people in your life (**Wǒ de péngyou shuō yìdiǎn Yìdàlìyǔ.**)

> **'Me-specific' phrases**
> Wǒ xǐhuan ...
>
> Wǒ yào ...
>
> Wǒ de péngyou ...
> _____ _____
>
> _____ _____

GETTING READY FOR YOUR FIRST CONVERSATION

I highly suggest having your first few conversations online with video enabled. Technology really is your friend in this situation. In an online chat, you can easily refer to your notes, and you can even look up words on the spot or put phrases you need into an online translator – right in the middle of the conversation.

I prefer to use automatic translation as a crutch, and never as a replacement for language learning.

Know this: if all else fails, you can have an entire conversation in Mandarin even if you only know these three phrases: **Wǒ bù míngbai. Xiě xiàlái. Qǐng děng yíxià.** Don't believe me? Envision it. Worst case scenario:

Your conversation partner says **Nǐ hǎo**, you say **Nǐ hǎo** (success!). But then she says, **@yego^3*8ham#3pt9ane1&?** And your mind goes blank.

You reply with **Wǒ bù míngbai. Xiě xiàlái.**

She types out what she said and sends it to you via chat. You select what she wrote, copy it and paste it and quickly find a translation. Ah, you think, I understand! But now it's your turn to respond, and your mind, again, goes blank.

You say, **Qǐng děng yíxià**! She waits patiently while you type what you want to say in English into your online translator. You hit enter and get a translation in Chinese. You read out the words in your best Mandarin accent.

Rinse and repeat.

Is this scenario ideal? No. But is it better than not having a conversation at all? Absolutely.

In fact, you'd be surprised by how much you'd learn even in this worst-case scenario. Even if you forgot every single phrase you learned in Chinese except these three, you could have a conversation (of sorts) in Chinese with another person. And you would learn loads of Chinese by the end of it.

Luckily, you've already been preparing for this moment for the past nine missions. So you're ready – even if you think you're not. Trust me on this.

Here's how I suggest you set yourself up for your conversation.

- Open up your cheat sheet and keep it within easy view.
- Have your translation tool ready (see our recommended Resources).
- Get ready to connect the call.
- Just before your conversation, practice listening to and repeating some Chinese audio.

WHAT TO EXPECT

During this conversation, don't focus on saying things perfectly. Being understood is the main goal here. Don't stress about knowing all the grammar, using precisely the right word or having a perfect accent.

Your purpose is to learn, practice and gain confidence. If you remember this, you can't fail. You'll have plenty of time to improve and impress in later conversations.

> **CONVERSATION STRATEGY:** *handling your nerves*
> It's typical for a beginner to expect to be judged by the other speaker. If you find yourself staring at the screen, afraid to push that Call button – and we've all been there – have a friend nearby to boost your confidence. Don't worry! The other person is probably just as nervous as you!
> A language-exchange partner may be worried more about how their English sounds than how you sound speaking Mandarin! And a new teacher may be hoping to make a good first impression!

Let's review some of the skills you've learned throughout this book.

Rephrasing – Take many of the phrases you ideally want to say, and simplify them. This is an essential skill for language hackers.

'Tarzan Mandarin' – Don't be afraid to speak in 'Tarzan Mandarin'! If you know how to say something right, say it right. But if you know how to say something kind of wrong, then say it wrong! Your language partner will help you figure out the wording you need.

Learn from your gaps – Despite rephrasing, you'll realize there's still a lot you don't yet know how to say. And as you talk, you'll realize you've been pronouncing some words wrong. Your partner may correct you. Good! This is valuable information. Take notes!

When in doubt, guess! – Finally, if you're not sure what your conversation partner just said, guess! Use context to infer the meaning of the entire phrase.

Talking one-on-one with another person is the best language practice you can get. If there's one secret to #languagehacking, this is it. Enjoy your first conversation, and the many others to come after that!

> Remember that perfectionism is your enemy in language learning. If you guess right, the conversation will advance, and if you guess wrong, you'll have had an opportunity to learn something new. And that's what this is all about!
>
> Don't take corrections personally. Appreciate them as they help you improve.

COMPLETING UNIT 10

Check your understanding

One mission left to go! Review the phrases and conversation strategies from the unit one more time. When you're feeling confident, listen to the audio rehearsal, which will help you practice your listening, pronunciation and speaking skills.

Practice answering common questions.

1 ◀ŷ) **10.02 Listen to the audio rehearsal, which will ask questions in Mandarin.**

···⋗ Practice answering the questions by giving spoken responses in Mandarin that are true for you.
···⋗ Pause or replay the audio as often as you need.
···⋗ Practice listening to someone describe herself.

> **CONVERSATION STRATEGY:**
> *warm up before your first conversation!*
> Practicing with audio is one of the best ways to prepare for a conversation. It will get your ears and your tongue 'warmed up' for the conversation. An hour or two before your Mandarin conversation begins, come back to these exercises and replay them to help you get into the flow of Chinese.

This is exactly what you'll be doing in your first conversation – listening to your partner and using a combination of your new #languagehacking skills and context to help you through even the tricky parts.

2 🔊 **10.03** In this audio rehearsal, a Mandarin speaker talks casually about herself. Listen to the audio, and after each clip, use what you understand (or can infer) to answer questions about the speaker.

⋯⟫ What is her name?
⋯⟫ Where is she from?
⋯⟫ Where does she live now?
⋯⟫ How long has she been teaching Mandarin?
⋯⟫ Does she speak any other languages? If so, which ones?
⋯⟫ What are some of the things she's interested in?

Show what you know...

Before your final mission, make sure that you:

☐ Write up the essential phrases you'll need into your cheat sheet.
☐ Write up survival phrases and add them to your cheat sheet.
☐ Prepare 2–5 'me-specific' phrases you want to practice. Add them to your cheat sheet.
☐ Prepare at least three questions you plan to ask. Add them to your cheat sheet.

Don't forget, whether it's learning new phrases, or improving your pronunciation, it's always OK to ask directly for the help you need!

What are your goals?

Know what you want to accomplish or what phrases you'd like to practice. Be realistic, but ambitious! And be flexible – you never know where a conversation will take you, and that's a very good thing for language learners. Write out a few notes on what you want to practice during your first conversation, or create your own bingo sheet! Then, find your language partner.

zhēn de ma?		Wǒ èrshí suì de shíhou...	
wǒ xǐhuan	Zài wǒ kànlái		Lǎoshí shuō – Wǒ suǒ zhīdao de
zuótiān jīntiān míngtiān	Wǒ yǐjing gàosu nǐ le ma?	Shénme? Shéi? Zài nǎ lǐ? Jǐ ge / Duōshao?	
yì diǎn	Yǒushí		Kāichē – Zuò bāshì

Many learners like to set up 'conversation bingo' when practicing a language online. To play, you write out a few phrases you want to practice during the call (either by speaking them or hearing them) and try to cross off as many as you can.

COMPLETE YOUR MISSION

It's time to complete your mission: having a one-on-one conversation with a native ... online. To do this, you'll need to prepare to:

⋯⟩ say hello and use essential greeting vocabulary
⋯⟩ ask at least three questions
⋯⟩ give your answers to commonly asked questions
⋯⟩ use survival phrases when you can't understand or need help
⋯⟩ say goodbye or set up a time to talk again.

STEP 1: find your conversation partner and schedule your first conversation

Follow our Resources to find a conversation partner online and schedule your first chat with them now.

When you're setting up your first conversation online, the first thing to do is send out a few messages to the exchange partners or teachers who look like a good fit for you. Break the ice and send them a message (in Chinese of course!) to set up your first chat. A good icebreaker tells the other person:

⋯⟩ your name and Chinese level
⋯⟩ what you'd like to practice or discuss during the conversation.

Here's an example:

Nǐ hǎo! Wǒ jiào Leigh. Wǒ kěyǐ gēn nǐ shuō Zhōngwén ma? Nǐ jiào shénme míngzi? Wǒ xiǎng liànxí jiǎndān de jùzi. Lìrú shuō, wǒ xiǎng shuō wǒ de míngzi hé wǒ de guójiā. Wǒ gānggāng kāishǐ xué Zhōngwén. Wǒmen míngtiān kěyǐ liáotiān ma? – Xièxie nǐ.

HACK IT: *time pressure is your friend*
Schedule it for tomorrow or the earliest possible slot. Don't give yourself a long window to get ready – overthinking this step can lead to procrastination later. Make a request for the next time slot, and don't look back!

Be friendly, and give a short introduction to yourself and what you want to practice – but don't say too much! Save some phrases for the conversation. Write out your own icebreaker now.

STEP 2: go all the way ... online

The first time might be scary, but it will get easier! Go online and have your first conversation in Mandarin for an authentic experience and good time!

Here's what to do during your conversation:

···⫶ Practice rephrasing your thoughts into simple forms.
···⫶ Speak 'Tarzan Mandarin' if you have to – it's better than nothing!
···⫶ Take note of any gaps in your Chinese vocabulary.
···⫶ Write down any phrases or words you want to say, but don't know yet.
···⫶ Write down new words or phrases you want to review later.

STEP 3: learn from other learners, and share your experience!

Tell the community how it went. (Or, if you're nervous, head over to see how other people's first conversations went.) Your task is to ask or answer at least three questions from other learners:

···⫶ Were you nervous? How did you handle your nerves?
···⫶ What was your teacher or exchange partner like?
···⫶ What went well? What didn't? What would you do differently next time?

STEP 4: reflect on what you've learned

After your first conversation, it's easy to focus on the words you didn't know or the things you couldn't say. But it's much more productive to focus on your successes instead. Were you 'only' able to give your name and your job, and say that you live with your cat? Those are huge wins!

Don't overlook your achievements.

What were your wins? What phrases were you able to say or understand?

Review the notes you took during your conversation. What words did you need that you don't know yet? What new words did you learn?

Remember, your first conversation is just that – a first conversation. The only way to get to your 50th conversation is to get the first one out of the way, then keep going from there.

As for the words you didn't know – that's one major benefit of having one-on-one conversations! You learn very quickly where the gaps are in your script, so you can work on filling them.

HEY, LANGUAGE HACKER, YOU JUST HAD A CONVERSATION IN CHINESE!

Or at least you should have!

You just broke one of the biggest barriers in language learning! Now that you've crossed that threshold, you are on a fast track to fluency in Mandarin that most people only ever dream about. Enjoy this milestone.

And remember – your second conversation will be even better than your first. Your third will be even better than that. Schedule your next spoken lesson now – don't put it off – that ticking clock is a powerful motivator for language hackers.

Your next mission: **Jiāyóu!** Keep it up!

ANSWER KEY

UNIT 1

CONVERSATION 1

Figure it out   **1** hello (literally 'you good')
2 wǒ shì **3** Wǒ hěn gāoxìng rènshi nǐ.   **4** I wǒ;
you nǐ

Practice   **1** a. hěn b. shì c. shì d. hěn
e. hěn f. shì **2** wéi **3** a. nǐ you b. hǎo good
4 ma **5** a. Nǐ shì Wáng Xiānsheng ma? b. Nǐ
shì xuésheng ma? **6** a. Nǐ zài ma? b. Nǐ shì
xuésheng ma? **7** a. Nǐ shi ... ma? Nǐ shi b. Nǐ zai,
Nǐ zai ... ma? **8** a. Wǒ shì Wáng Lǎoshī. b. Hěn
gāoxìng rènshi nǐ.

Pronunciation: Tones   **2** a. falling-rising
b. rising c. falling d. falling e. level f. rising

Put it together   Examples: Nǐ hǎo. Wǒ shì
Àilìsī. Wǒ hěn gāoxìng rènshi nǐ.

CONVERSATION 2

Figure it out   **1** They say 'I am' four times in
Conversation 2.

Wáng Lǎoshī :	Wǒ shì Zhōngguó rén. Lucy, nǐ shì nǎ guó rén?
Lucy :	Ā... **wǒ shì** Jiānádà rén.
Wáng Lǎoshī :	Wǒ zhù zài Běijīng. **Wǒ shì** Shànghǎi rén.
Lucy :	Duìbùqǐ... Wǒ bù míngbai. Nǐ zhù zài Shànghǎi ma?
Wáng Lǎoshī :	Wǒ zhù zài Běijīng. **Wǒ shì** Shànghǎi rén. Nǐ míngbai ma?
Lucy :	Ā, wǒ míngbai le.
Wáng Lǎoshī :	Lucy, nǐ zhù nǎli?
Lucy :	Wǒ zhù zài Zhījiāgē.

2 Wǒ zhù zài **3** Lucy lives in the US. / Zhījiāgē
4 Teacher Wang mentions Beijing and Shanghai.
He is from Shanghai, but he currently lives in
Beijing. / Běijīng; Shànghǎi **5** Wǒ bù míngbai

Notice   **2** a. Canada: Jiānádà b. person: rén
c. Canadian: Jiānádà rén d. China: Zhōngguó
e. person: rén f. Chinese: Zhōngguó rén
3 a. I am: wǒ shì b. I live in: wǒ zhù zài
c. I understand: wǒ míngbai d. I'm Canadian:
wǒ shì Jiānádà rén
4 a. You live in: Nǐ zhù zài b. You understand:
Nǐ míngbai c. You are: Nǐ shì
5 a. I'm not Chinese: Wǒ bú shì Zhōngguó rén
b. I don't understand: Wǒ bù míngbai c. You
don't understand: Nǐ bù míngbai d. You're
not: Nǐ bú shì
6 a. Where are you from?: Nǐ shì nǎ guó rén?
b. Where do you live?: Nǐ zhù zài nǎli?

Building 'me-specific' language   **1** Students'
own answers
2 a. Germany: Déguó b. Rome: Luómǎ
c. England: Yīngguó d. Sydney: Xīní e. from
Germany: Déguó rén f. from Rome: Luómǎ
rén g. from England: Yīngguó rén h. from
Sydney: Xīní rén
3 a. Wǒ shì Fǎguórén b. Wǒ zhù zài Fǎguó.
c. Mark shì Yīngguó rén. d. Mark zhù zài Yīngguó.
e. Wáng Lǎoshī shì Zhōngguó rén. f. Wǒ bú shì
Měiguó rén. g. Wǒ shì Ài'ěrlán rén. h. Nǐ zhù zài
Měiguó. i. Nǐ bú shì Xībānyá rén.

Put it together   **1** Examples: Wǒ shì Dàixī.
Wǒ shì Fǎguó rén. Wǒ zhù zài Déguó. (I'm Daisy.
I'm French. I live in Germany.) Wǒ shì Mǎlì. Wǒ
shì Rìběn rén. Wǒ zhù zài Hánguó. (I'm Mari. I am
Japanese. I live in Korea.) **2** Nǐ shì nǎ guó rén?;
Nǐ zhù zài nǎli?

UNDERSTANDING PINYIN PART 1

2 a. Q (qín) **b.** X (xīn) **c.** Zh (zhōng) **d.** R (rén) **e.** S (sòng) **f.** J (jiào) **g.** Sh (shì) **h.** Z (zào) **i.** C (cuò) **j.** Ch (chào)

MISSION SCRIPT – MODEL

Step 1 Nǐ hǎo. Wǒ shì Jímǔ. Wǒ shì Yīngguó rén. Wǒ zhù zài Ài'ěrlán.

UNIT 2

CONVERSATION 1

Figure it out 1 a. three **b.** bú shì (no) **c.** two **2 a.** duì **b.** duì **c.** duì **d.** duì **3** huì bu huì **4** Nǐ ne? **5** nà

Notice 1 Wǒ zhǐ huì shuō Yīmgyǔ, yìdiǎn Zhōngwén. **2 a.** yìdiǎn **b.** yíxià **c.** yíxià **3 a.** Not yet: Hài bú huì **b.** Not bad: bú cuò **c.** Also: yě **d.** May I ask: Qǐngwèn **4** huì **5 a.** shì, am **b.** bú shì, am not **c.** míngbai, understand **d.** bù míngbai, don't understand **e.** huì shuō, can speak **f.** bú huì shuō, can't speak **g.** yào, want **h.** bú yào, don't want

Grammar explanation: asking questions
1 a. nǐ míngbai, you understand **b.** Nǐ míngbai ma?, Do you understand? **c.** Wǒ yào, I want **d.** Wǒ yào ma?, Do I want? **e.** Lucy huì shuō Zhōngwén., Lucy can speak Chinese. **f.** Lucy huì shuō Zhōngwén ma?, Can Lucy speak Chinese? **2 a.** Nǐ shì Měiguó rén., You are American. **b.** Nǐ shì Měiguó rén, shì bu shì?, You are American, aren't you? **c.** Nǐ zhù zài Běijīng., You live in Bejing. **d.** Nǐ zhù zài Běijīng, shì bu shì?, You live in Beijing, don't you? **e.** Lucy liànxí yíxià., Lucy practices a bit. **f.** Lucy liànxí yíxià, shì bu shì?, Lucy practices a bit, doesn't she? **3 a.** Wǒ shì Fǎguó rén. Nǐ ne? **b.** Wǒ zhù zài Déguó. Nǐ ne? **c.** Wǒ shì George. Nǐ ne?

Practice 1 a. shì **b.** huì **c.** bú **d.** yíxià **e.** shì bu shì **2 a.** D **b.** W **c.** W **d.** D **e.** W **f.** D

Put it together 1 a. Rìyǔ **b.** Déyǔ **c.** Fǎyǔ **d.** Éyǔ **e, f.** Students' own answers **2** Students' own answers

CONVERSATION 2

Figure it out 1 a. Xǐhuan. **b.** Zhōngwén (Chinese), Rìyǔ (Japanese), Éyǔ (Russian) **2 a.** Qǐngwèn **b.** Tài bàng le! **c.** tiǎozhàn **3** yes

Notice 1 Qǐngwèn **2 a.** xué **b.** xǐhuan **3** 3; Zhōngwén, Rìyǔ, Éyǔ; Chinese, Japanese, Russian **4 a.** Hái xíng ba. **b.** bú cuò **c.** hěn nán

Practice 1 2 duō jiǔ le **3 a.** yǐjing **b.** Zhǐ yǒu **c.** hái xíng ba **5 b.** three weeks: sān ge xīngqī **c.** six months: liù ge yuè **d.** eight months: bā ge yuè **e.** ten years: shí nián **f.** five days: wǔ tiān

Practice 2 1 a. Wǒ yǐjing xué Zhōngwén xué le sān ge yuè le. **b.** Nǐ zhù zài Běijīng duō jiǔ le? **c.** Wǒ zhèngzài xué Éyǔ hé Fǎyǔ. **2** Students' own answers

Practice 3 Students' answers will vary.

Building 'me-specific' language Table: Hányǔ, Éyǔ, Zhōngwén, Déyǔ, Fǎyǔ

Put it together Examples: Wǒ yǐjing xué le shísì tiān le. Wǒ huì shuō Yīngyǔ hé Fǎyǔ. Wǒ sānshí suì. Wǒ xué le yí ge xīngqī le. Wǒ huì shuō Xiōngyálìyǔ (Hungarian). Wǒ èrshí sì suì.

UNDERSTANDING PINYIN PART 2

2 a. p **b.** g **c.** b **d.** m **e.** n **f.** g **g.** d **h.** l **i.** t **j.** k **k.** h

MISSION SCRIPT – MODEL

Nǐ huì shuō Yīngyǔ. Nǐ xué le duōjiǔ le? Qǐngwèn, nǐ xǐhuan xué yǔyán, shì bu shì? Wǒ yǐjing xué le sān ge yuè le. Wǒ yě huì shuō Xībānyáyǔ. Wǒ de Xībānyáyǔ bú cuò. Wǒ yě yào xué Yìdàlìyǔ.

UNIT 3

CONVERSATION 1

Figure it out   **1** c **2** a. méi wèntí **b.** gàosu wǒ ba **c.** duìbùqǐ **3** I can't hear: wǒ tīng bú dào; Can you hear?: Nǐ tīng de dào ma? **4** 'Qǐng zài shuō yíbiàn' means 'Please say it again' in English'.

Practice   **1** màn yìdiǎn **2** shénme **3** a. gāoxìng **b.** Qǐng **c.** ne **4** a. shuō: (to) say/speak **b.** tīng: (to) hear/listen **c.** gàosu: (to) tell **d.** yǒu: (to) have **e.** xǐhuan: (to) like

Conversation strategy: learn set phrases
1 a. ma **b.** ma **c.** ma **d.** ma **e.** ma **f.** ne **2** a. 5 **b.** 4 **c.** 6 **d.** 3 **e.** 1 **f.** 2 **3** a. hěn **b.** yìdiǎn **c.** shénme **d.** xiànzài

Grammar explanation: repeated verbs
1 Nǐ wánwan ba. **2** Qǐng xuéxíxuéxí Zhōngwén. **3** Nǐ wènwen.

Put it together   Examples:
⋯⟫ Wǒ jiào Dàixī. (My name is Daisy.)
⋯⟫ Wǒ xǐhuan tī zúqiú. (I like to play soccer.)
⋯⟫ Wǒ yě liàn wǔshù. (I also do martial arts.)
⋯⟫ Wǒ bù xǐhuan dǎ bàngqiú. (I don't like playing baseball.)
⋯⟫ Wǒ bù xǐhuan chī là de shíwù. (I don't like to eat spicy food.)

CONVERSATION 2

Figure it out   **1** a. duì **b.** cuò **c.** duì **2** a. Nǐ xǐhuān shénme yīnyuè? **b.** Lǎoshī shuō **3** Hěn yǒu yìsi. / yǒu **4** a. Hái tīng bú dào. (I still don't hear.) **b.** Nǐ bù xǐhuan shénme yīnyuè? (You don't like what music?) **c.** Zhēn de ma? (Really?) **5** Students' own answers

Notice   **2** a. tīng **b.** xué **c.** liànxí **3** a. Nǐ yào liánxi yíxià. **b.** Wǒ yào děng. **c.** Wǒ yào zhù zài Běijīng. **d.** Lucy yào xué Zhōngwén. **e.** Jùnfēng yào wán diànzǐ yóuxì. **f.** Nǐ yào tīng yīnyuè.
4 a. Duìbùqǐ. **b.** Wǒ bù míngbai. **c.** Zhēn de ma? **d.** Qǐng zài shuō yíbiàn. **e.** Qǐng děng yíxià. **f.** Hái bù míngbai.

Your turn: use the hack   **1** a. 3 **b.** 1 **c.** 5 **d.** 2 **e.** 6 **f.** 7 **g.** 4 **h.** 8

Tarzan Mandarin   **1** a. Duìbùqǐ, qǐng màn yìdian zài shuō yíbiàn. - Qǐng, yíbiàn. **b.** Qǐng gàosu wǒ, zhè ge duōshao qián? - Duōshao? **c.** Qǐng wèn, nǐ zhīdao chāoshì zài nǎli ma? - Chāoshì zài nǎli?

Practice

Meaning	Chinese	Meaning	Chinese
Why?	Wéishénme?	Who?	Shéi?
What?	Shénme?	How long?	Duōjiǔ?
How?	Zěnme?	How much?	Duōshao?
Where?	Zài nǎli?	How is?	Zěnmeyàng?
When?	Shénme shíhou?		

2 a. Shénme shíhou? **b.** Duōshao qián? **c.** Shéi **d.** Zài nǎli? **e.** Shénme? **3** a. wèishénme **b.** shénme **c.** shénme shíhou **d.** shéi **e.** zài nǎli **f.** zěnmeyàng **4** a. zài nǎli **b.** shénme **c.** wéishénme **d.** zěnmeyàng **e.** shénme

Grammar explanation: 'le'–the past tense?
1 a. Wǒ xué le Fǎyǔ. **b.** Wǒ měitiān liànxí le. **c.** Wǒ xǐhuan jīngjù le.

Understanding Pinyin: the final sounds
2 a. fù **b.** guó **c.** táng **d.** bào **e.** lùn **f.** èr **g.** cì **h.** le **i.** mén **j.** liù **k.** fàn **l.** jiě **m.** fēi **n.** mā **o.** jiào **p.** huà **q.** mín **r.** yuán **s.** gǒu **t.** lái **u.** fēng **v.** jiā **w.** jiàn **x.** shuài

COMPLETE YOUR MISSION

Build your script   Example: Nǐ hǎo, wǒ jiào Milo. Wǒ shì Měiguó rén. Wǒ xǐhuan yùndòng. Wǒ yě xǐhuan yóuxì. Dànshì wǒ bù xǐhuan gāo'ěrfū. Wǒ xǐhuan tīng juéshìyuè. Wǒ bù xǐhuan liúxíng yīnyuè. (Hello, my name is Milo. I am American. I like sports. I also like games. But I don't like golf. I like to listen to jazz. I don't like popular music.)

MISSION SCRIPT – MODEL

Tāmen shì gēshǒu. Tāmen shì Yīngguó rén. Tāmen hěn yǒumíng. Yǒu sì ge rén. Tāmen chàng 'Eleanor Rigby'.

UNIT 4

CONVERSATION 1

Figure it out   **1 a.** gēge **b.** xiōngdì jiěmèi **c.** dìdi **d.** mèimei **2 a.** What is his name? Tā jiào shénme míngzi? **b.** His name is ... Tā jiào ... **c.** Do you have siblings? Nǐ yǒu xiōngdì jiěmèi ma? **d.** ...lives with my parents gēn wǒ de fùmǔ zhù zài yìqǐ **e.** married jiéhūn **3 a.** Lǐwèi lives in Guangzhou. (Tiānjīn) **b.** Ann lives with Lucy's parents. (David) **c.** Lǐwèi doesn't have children. (has) **d.** Xiǎowēi is going to hang out with her brother next weekend. (hung out last weekend) **4 a.** last weekend: shàng zhōumò **b.** lately: zuìjìn **c.** now: xiànzài **d.** today: jīntiān **e.** already: yǐjīng **5** Tā yǒu liǎng ge háizi. She has two children/kids.

Notice   **1 a.** Wǒ de mèimei gēn wǒ de fùmǔ zhù zài yìqǐ. **b.** Wǒ de gēge jiéhūn le. **c.** Wǒ méiyǒu dìdi. **d.** Wǒ gēn wǒ de xiōngdì zhù zài yìqǐ. **2 a.** tā **b.** tā **c.** tāmen **d.** nǐ **e.** nǐmen **f.** wǒmen **3 a.** Nǐ méiyǒu jiějie. **b.** Wǒ bú shì dìdi. **c.** Wǒ yǒu liǎng ge xiōngdì. **d.** Tā gēn wǒ de

mèimei zhù zài yìqǐ. **e.** Wǒ yǒu dìdi, dànshì wǒ méiyǒu gēge.

Grammar explanation: gēn ... yìqǐ   **a.** gēn wǒ (de) fùmǔ yìqǐ **b.** gēn tā (de) jiějie yìqǐ **c.** gēn yí ge péngyou yìqǐ **d.** gēn tā (de) qīzi yìqǐ

Practice   **2** Student's answers **3 a** xiōngdì **b** érzi **c** péngyou **d** māma **e** fùmǔ **4** Students' answers will vary.

Vocab tip   **a.** wǒ de māma de jiějie de nǚ'ér **b.** wǒ de bàba de bàba **c.** wǒ de māma de bàba de gēge

Put it together   **1** Example: Wǒ zhù zài Niǔyuē. Wǒ de jiārén zhù zài Ài'ěrlán. Wǒ dìdi shì yīnyuè rén. Tā tán gāngqín. **2** Wǒ péngyou jiào Mǎtè. Tā xǐhuan lǚxíng.

CONVERSATION 2

Figure it out   **1 a.** Wǒmen **b.** zhù zài **c.** yào **2 a.** Xiǎowēi / xīn péngyou **b.** Yíhéyuán **c.** Běijīng kǎoyā **d.** Zhōngguó Tiānjīn rén

Notice   **1 a.** xièxie **b.** dànshì **c.** zuò **d.** jiārén **e.** nǚpéngyou **f.** kàn **2 a.** wǒ de xīn péngyou **b.** zhè ge xīngqī **c.** zhè ge xīngqī nèi **d.** kěnéng **e.** dāngrán xūyào **3 a.** míngzi **b.** zuò **c.** Míngtiān **d.** kěnéng **e.** xiǎng

Practice   Students' answers will vary.

#LANGUAGEHACK

Your turn: use the hack   **1 a.** buying a new computer **b.** visiting a friend in Australia **c.** getting married **d.** learning Spanish **2 a.** wǒ yào xuéxí Déyǔ **b.** dǎ lánqiú **c.** méi yǒu gēge **3** Students' answers may vary. Example: Zhè zhōumò wǒ gēn wǒ de gēge yìqǐ chūqù wán. Wǒmen qù kàn diànyǐng. Ránhòu, wǒmen qù yèshì chīfàn. (This weekend, I am going out with my older brother. We are going to see a movie. Then we are going to the night market to eat.) 4. Students' answers may vary. Example: Rúguǒ nǐ xiǎng qù, nǐ yīnggāi qù. (If you want to go, then you should go.) Wǒ hē kāfēi jiā niúnǎi, dànshì qǐng bù jiā táng. (I drink my coffee with milk, but please don't add sugar.)

Put it together   Wǒ de jiā yǒu sì ge rén - wǒ de zhàngfū hé wǒ de háizi. Wǒ yǒu yí ge nǚ'ér hé yí ge érzi. Wǒ érzi xǐhuān gōngfū. Wǒ de nǚ'ér xǐhuān yīnyuè. Wǒmen zhù zài Jiāzhōu.

CHARACTERS

男人   Check your understanding
⋯⇥ Nǐ de jiā yǒu hěnduō rén ma? Yǒu. Wǒ de jiā yǒu hěnduō rén.
⋯⇥ Nǐ gēn nǐ de fùmǔ zhù zài yìqǐ ma? Shì. Wǒ gēn wǒ de fùmǔ zhù zài yìqǐ.
⋯⇥ Nǐ yǒu xiōngdì jiěmèi ma? Yǒu. Wǒ yǒu xiōngdì jiěmèi.
⋯⇥ Nǐ de gēge jiéhūn le ma? Wǒ de gēge jiéhūn le.
⋯⇥ Tā yǒu háizi ma? Yǒu. Tā yǒu háizi.
⋯⇥ Tāmen xǐhuān shénme? Tāmen xǐhuān yùndòng.

MISSION SCRIPT – MODEL

Tā shì wǒ de érzi. Tā hěn cōngmíng. Wǒmen yìqǐ wán. Tā sì suì. Tā hàixiū. Tā xǐhuān yùndòng. Tā xǐhuan lǜsè. Tā bù xǐhuan huàhuà.

UNIT 5

CONVERSATION 1

Figure it out   **1 a.** (Qǐng wèn,) nín huì shuō Zhōngwén ma? **b.** Táiwān **2 a.** Wǒ shì Táiwān rén. **b.** Wǒ gēn nín shuō Zhōngwén, kěyǐ ma? **c.** Dànshì nǐ shuō Zhōngwén shuō de hěn hǎo. **d.** Wǒmen kāishǐ ba! **3** Wǒ shì gānggang kāishǐ de. **4 a.** together: yìqǐ **b.** can: kěyǐ **c.** really: zhēnde **5 a.** Tài hǎo le! **b.** Méi wèntí! **c.** Zhēnde!

Conversation strategy: introducing yourself   **1 a.** Qǐngwèn, nín huì shuō Zhōngwén ma? **b.** Wǒ gēn nín shuō Zhōngwén, kěyǐ ma? **2 a.** 3 **b.** 1 **c.** 2 **d.** 4

Grammar explanation: adverbs   **1** shuō de hěn kuài **2** chī de hěn hǎo **3** shuō de bú màn

Practice   **1 a.** yào **b.** yào **c.** xiǎng **2 a.** Wǒ xiǎng qù Xī'ān. **b.** Wǒ yào shuǐ. **c.** Wǒ yào xué. **d.** Wǒ xiǎng wǒ (de) māma. **e.** Wǒ yào qù Guilin.

Grammar explanation: word order
1 Students' answers will vary. **2 a** Jīnnián wǒ zài Běijīng xué leliù ge yuè. **b** Nǐ xīngqīwǔ zài fànguǎn chī. **c** Wǒmen měinián zài Xiānggǎng gōngzuò yícì.

Put it together   **1** Students' answers may vary. Examples: Wǒ yào gēn nǐ shuōhuà, kěyǐ ma? (I want to talk to you, could I?), Wǒ xiǎng zuò zài zhèlǐ, kěyǐ ma? (I would like to sit here, can I?) **2** Students' answers may vary. Example: Nǐ huì shuō Zhōngwén ma? Wǒ yě huì shuō! Nǐ yào yìqǐ liànxí ma? (You can speak Chinese? I can too! Do you want to practice together?)

CONVERSATION 2

Figure it out   **1 a.** Nǐ shi shénme shíhou lái dào Běijīng de? **b.** sān ge yuè qián **c.** Shì de. **2** Nǐ de yìsi shì **3 a.** Lucy wants to go to Japan after China. **b.** Wǎntíng suggests that Lucy visit Taiwan. **4 a.** piàoliang **b.** kěnéng **c.** duō **d.** qítā **5** Lìrú

Notice   **1** Wǒ de yìsi shì **2** Nǐ de yìsi shì **3 a.** dōngxi **b.** shìqing or dōngxi **c.** dōngxi **4 a.** 3 **b.** 4 **c.** 1 **d.** 5 **e.** 6 **f.** 2 **5 a.** maybe **b.** before **c.** other **d.** so much **e.** even more

Pronunciation explanation: tone changes
2 a. yí bàn **b.** bú shì **c.** yíyàng **d.** yǔfǎ

Put it together   Example: Wǒ chángcháng lǚxíng. Jīnnián chūntiān, wǒ qù Tèlāwéifū. Wǒ zài nàlǐ dāi yí ge xīngqī. Wǒ zuò fēijī qù Tèlāwéifū. (I often travel. This spring, I am going to Tel Aviv. I will stay there one week. I will take a plane to go to Tel Aviv.)

MISSION SCRIPT – MODEL

Wǒ huì qù Dōngjīng. Wǒ yào chī hěnduō Rìběn liàolǐ. Xiàtiān, wǒ hé jiārén yìqǐ qù. Wǒmen dāi yí ge xīngqī. Wǒmen zài Dōngjīng zuò dìtiě. (I am going to Tokyo. I want to eat lots of Japanese food. Next summer, I am going with my family. We will stay there one week. We will take the subway in Tokyo.)

UNIT 6

CONVERSATION 1

Nǐmen yào diǎn shénme?

Figure it out   1   a. liǎng wèi **b.** liǎng ge rén **c.** Wǒ dùzi è le **d.** zhè shì càidān **2** What do you want to order? **3   a.** yì wǎn zhájiàngmiàn **b.** yì pán xīhóngshì chǎo jīdàn **c.** yì wǎn suānlà tāng **d.** yì bēi rè shuǐ **4   a.** Wǒ mǎshàng huílái. **b.** hěn là ma

Notice   1 In Chinese, the phrase for 'I'm hungry' is 'I stomach hungry'. In Chinese, the reference to 'stomach' is added. **2   a.** yì wǎn **b.** yì pán **b.** yì bēi **3   a.** rè **b.** zhǔnbèi **c.** là **4   a.** 6 **b.** 3 **c.** 9 **d.** 1 **e.** 2 **f.** 10 **g.** 7 **h.** 4 **i.** 8 **j.** 5

Practice   1   a. Nǐ yào diǎn shénme? **b.** Wǒ yào yì bēi rè chá. **c.** Wǒ yào yì wǎn suānlà tāng. **d.** Wǒ bù xǐhuan là. **e.** Wǒ bù néng chī là de. **f.** Nǐ dùzi è le ma?

Put it together   1   a. Example: Wǒ yào Běijīng kǎoyā. (I want Beijing duck.) **b.** Hái yào yì pán suānlà tǔdòu sī. (I'd also like potato stir

fry.) **c.** Yì bēi hóngchá. (One cup of black tea.) **d.** Fúwùyuán! **e.** Zài yào yì bēi hóngchá. (I want another cup of black tea.) **2** Example: Wǒ chī pīsà. Wǒ hē kāfēi. Wǒ měitiān zuòfàn. (I eat pizza. I drink coffee. I cook every day.)

CONVERSATION 2

Lucy and Xiǎowēi compromise. First they'll visit the Great Wall. After lunch, they'll go to the Forbidden City. Then they'll go to hutongs.

Figure it out   1   a. Chángchéng (The Great Wall), Gùgōng (The Forbidden City) **b.** Rénshānrénhǎi **c.** Gùgōng méiyǒu Chángchéng de rén duō. Gùgōng méiyǒu Chángchéng de měi jǐng. **d.** tuōxié **2   a.** I don't agree: wǒ bù tóngyì **b.** not true: búshì zhēn de. **c.** a little boring: yǒudiǎn wúliáo **d.** then: ránhòu **3   a.** person **b.** must-see **c.** a little **d.** compromise

Notice   1   a. gèng hǎo **b.** dōu **c.** fēicháng **2   a.** yǒu yìsi **b.** měi **3   a.** gèng jījí **b.** gèng měi **c.** gèng yǒu yìsi **4   a.** Wǒ juéde **b.** Wǒ juéde tāng gèng hǎo. **c.** Wǒ juéde nàli zǒng shì rénshānrénhǎi. **5   a.** 5 **b.** 4 **c.** 7 **d.** 2 **e.** 6 **f.** 3 **g.** 1 **h.** 8

Grammar explanation: comparisons Practice   1   a. Wǒ de shū méiyǒu nǐ de shū lǎo. **b.** Wǒ méiyǒu tā shīwàng. **c.** Wǒ de mèimei méiyǒu wǒ de jiějie gāo. **d.** Wǒ juéde wǒ méiyǒu wǒ de māma piàoliang. **e.** Wǒ méiyǒu wǒ de dìdi cōngming. **2   a.** zuì cōngming **b.** Shànghǎi hé Běijīng yíyàng piàoliang. **c.** gèng lèi **3   a.** méiyǒu **b.** zuì **c.** yíyàng **d.** gèng

Put it together   Example: Wǒ xiǎng qù Shànghǎi. Wǒ rènwéi zhè shì Zhōngguó zuì měilì de chéngshì. Gòuwù shì zuì hǎo de!

COMPLETING UNIT 6

Check your understanding   a. cuò **b.** cuò **c.** cuò

MISSION SCRIPT – MODEL

Wǒ zuì xǐhuān de fàndiàn yǒu Rìběn liàolǐ. Wǒ xǐhuān shòusī. Wǒ xǐhuān chīyú. Chīyú duì shēntǐ jiànkāng yǒu hǎochù. Ròu méiyǒu yú yǒu wèidào. (My favorite restaurant has Japanese food. I like sushi. I like to eat fish. Fish is good for your body's health. Meat doesn't have fish's flavor.)

Notice 3

Dictionary form	Chinese – Past tense phrase	Meaning
zuò (to do/to make)	Nǐ zuò shénme le?	What did you do?
	a. Wǒmen zuò le (lǎo cù huā shēng).	We made (vinegar peanuts).
chī wǎnfàn (to eat dinner)	**b.** Wǒmen chī wǎnfàn le.	We ate dinner.
chī (to eat)	**c.** Wǒ chī le.	I ate.
shuō (to talk)	**d.** Wǒmen shuō le.	We talked.
kàndào (to see)	**e.** Wǒmen kàndào le …	We saw …
jiàndào (to meet)	**f.** Nǐ jiàndào (tā) le.	You met (her).
pāi zhàopiàn (to take photos)	**g.** Wǒmen pāi zhàopiàn le.	We took photos.
cānguān (to visit / to sight-see)	**h.** Wǒ cānguān le …	I visited …
xǐhuān (to like)	**i.** Xǐhuān le ma?	Did you like it?
	j. Wǒ xǐhuān le!	I liked it!

Figure it out   1 a. shàng zhōumò **b.** Zuótiān wǒmen kàndào... **c.** Zěnmeyàng? **d.** Hěn hǎo wán! **e.** Sì nián qián, **f.** chī le yì pán lǎo cù huāshēng **2 b 3 a.** cuò **b.** duì **c.** cuò **d.** duì **4** Yí ge rén means 'alone' or 'one person' **5 a.** jìhuà **b.** huìhuà **c.** tèbié

Notice   4 a. Sān tiān qián **b.** Sì tiān qián **c.** Shí fēnzhōng qián

Grammar explanation: forming the past with verbal complements   a. zuò wán **b.** chī bǎo **c.** zhǎo dào **d.** chī wán **e.** dào

UNIT 7

CONVERSATION 1

Nǐ shàng zhōumò zuò shénme le?

Notice   1 a. Nǐ shàng zhōumò zuò shénme le? **b.** Xiǎowēi hé wǒ yìqǐ chūqù wán le. **c.** Wǒmen yě tǎolùn le wǒmen zhōumò de jìhuà. **2 a.** shàng zhōumò **b.** yìqǐ **c.** zhōumò de jìhuà

Practice   a. Fànguǎn hěn hǎo. Liǎng tiān qián wǒ zài zhè'er chī le. **b.** Tā hé tā de dìdi qù Dūbólín le. **c.** Wǒ jīntiān kànwán shū le.

CONVERSATION 2

Nǐ zhè ge xīngqī xué Zhōngwén le ma?

Figure it out   1 a. Lucy practiced one sentence with Xiǎowēi. jǐ **b.** Lucy began learning Chinese several weeks ago. Yí ge yuè **c.** Lucy bought a ticket to go to Xi'an. Tiānjīn **2 a.** Lucy practiced some sentences with Xiǎowēi. **b.** I forgot! You already told me! **c.** Wǒ de fāyīn hǎo bu hǎo? **3 a.** difference **b.** I decide **c.** homework

Notice 1 a. I must say …: Wǒ bìxū shuō … **b.** I forgot!: Wǒ wàng le! **c.** Did you finish …?: Nǐ zuò wán **2** zhāng **3 a.** xué dào le **b.** lái guo **c.** zuò wán le **d.** tīng dào le **e.** mǎi le **f.** qù guo **g.** xúe le **h.** chī le

Grammar explanation: using guo for experiences 1 Tā yǐjing chī guo le. **2 a.** guo **b.** guo le **c.** guo; le

3 Past tense cheat sheet

1 Verbs	Past form	2 Verbs	Past experience
I spoke	shuō le	I spoke	shuō guo
I made	zuò le	I made	zuò guo
I bought	mǎi le	I bought	mǎi guo
I came	lái le	I came	lái guo
I studied	xué le	I studied	xué guo
I saw	kàn le	I saw	kàn guo
I ate	chī le	I ate	chī guo

Put it together 1 Example: Wǒ qù Élēgāng le. Wǒ shì sìyuè huílái de. Zhēn xǐhuān. Fēicháng piàoliang. **2** Example: Wǒ hé wǒ de jiārén qù lùyíng (camping). Shān (mountain[s]) hěn měi. Dànshì tiānqì (weather) hěn lěng (cold).

Your turn: use the hack 1 a. Wǒ xiànzài kàn diànyǐng. **b.** Wǒ míngtiān kàn diànyǐng. **c.** Wǒ shàng ge xīngqī kàn le zhè ge diànyǐng. **2** Example: Wǒ sān tiān qián zuò huǒchē. Wǒ kàn jiàn le yì zhī láng (a wolf). **3** Students' answers vary.

Put it together 1 Shàng ge xīngqi wǒ gēn xīn péngyou shuō Zhōngwén. Wǒ hěn jǐnzhāng. Dànshì wǒ péngyou shuō wǒ shuō de hěn hǎo. Wǒ hěn gāoxìng.

COMPLETING UNIT 7

Check your understanding 2 a. yǒu **b.** Tā yī gè rén lái le. **c.** Fǎguó **d.** Měiguó

UNIT 8

CONVERSATION 1

They use: Hǎojiǔ bújiàn! Zuìjìn hái hǎo ma? Suǒyǐ, gàosu wǒ ba, zuìjìn máng bu máng?

Figure it out 1 a. Wǒ měi ge xīngqī yǒu yì jié kè. **b.** Shàng cì wǒmen xué le zěnme zuò nǎi huáng bāo. **c.** Wǒ xiànzài zhèngzài xué zěnme zuò jiǎozi! **2 a.** gèng hǎo (better) **b.** chénggōng **c.** wēibōlú pīsà (microwave pizza) **3** Hǎojiǔ bújiàn! **4 a.** Lucy gānggāng kāishǐ xué zěnme zuòfàn. **b.** Lucy xiànzài zhèngzài xué zěnme zuò jiǎozi! **5 a.** Tīng dào **b.** Zuìjìn máng bu máng? **c.** Wǒ méiyǒu yíyàng de wèntí

Notice 1 Hǎojiǔ bújiàn! (Long time, no see!) Zuìjìn hái hǎo ma? (Have you been good lately?) **2 a.** wǒ gānggāng kāishǐ **b.** zhèngzài **c.** zuìjìn **d.** yǒudiǎn máng **e.** shàng cì **f.** kàn qǐlái **3 a.** xiànzài zhèngzài **b.** hěn kuài **c.** Zài jiā **d.** shíjiān wèntí. **4 a.** hǎo **b.** kāishǐ **c.** zuòfàn **5 a.** zěnme zuò **b.** zhèngzài xué zěnme **c.** gānggang kāishǐ xué

Conversation strategy: learn set phrases for each 'stage' of a conversation
1 a. fàn **b.** měi ge xīngqī yǒu yì jié kè **c.** zhèngzài xué zěnme zuò jiǎozi **2 a.** Lucy, nǐ hǎo! / Hǎojiǔ bújiàn! **b.** Zuìjìn hái hǎo ma? / Suǒyǐ, gàosu wǒ ba, zuìjìn máng bu máng? **c.** Zuìjìn wǒ gānggāng kāishǐ xué zěnme zuòfàn. / Shàng cì wǒmen xué le zěnme zuò nǎi huáng bāo. **d.** Wǒ rènzhēn yìdiǎn … jìxù ba. **3 a.** Wǒ zhīdao nǐ shì Yīngguó rén. **b.** Nǐ rènshì Sarah de xīn péngyou ma? **c.** Nǐ yǐjing kàn le zhè ge diànyǐng ma?

Put it together 1 Example: Wǒ gānggang kāishǐ xué gōngfu. Wǒ měi ge xīngqī qù liǎng cì. Wǒ zài jiā yě liànxí. Wǒ zhèngzài tígāo wǒ de shuǐpíng. (I just started kungfu. I go two times a week. I also practice at home. I'm in the middle of improving my level.) **2** Example: Wǒ kāishǐ shì yīnwèi wǒ yào yùndòng. Duì shēntǐ hěn hǎo. Dìyī cì shàng gōngfu kè yǐhòu, wǒ de liǎng tiáo tuǐ dōu suān le. Dànshì xiànzài wǒ hǎo le. (I started because I want to exercise. It's good for the body. The first time I attended the kungfu class, both of my legs were sore. But now I am fine.)

CONVERSATION 2

Lucy says **yǒudiǎn qíguài** to mean 'it was strange.' Taking a stroll helped Lucy get into the swing of things.

Figure it out 1

	goes for a walk before work	rides a bike	takes the car	always has lunch at a restaurant	sometimes tries new restaurants	prepares lunch at home
Lucy	✓	✓		✓		
Wǎntíng	✓	✓	✓		✓	✓

2 Zài wǒ kànlái, duì nǐ zài Běijīng yíqiè dōu hěn hǎo, duì bu duì? **3 a.** chū qù zài tā jiā fùjìn sànbù **b.** měitiān xiàwǔ **c.** dàochù **d.** Lucy xūyào xīnxiān kōngqì **e.** Wǎntíng kāichē

Notice 1 Duì nǐ láishuō zài Běijīng yìqiè dōu hěn hǎo, shì bú shì?

Notice 2

Time		Manner	Place
When?	**How often?**	**Why? / How?**	**Where?**
morning **a.** zǎoshang	often **e.** chángcháng	by car **k.** kāichē	in the park **m.** zài gōngyuán
afternoon **b.** xiàwǔ	sometimes **f.** yǒushí	by subway **l.** zuò dìtiě	everywhere **n.** dàochù
lunchtime/noon **c.** zhōngwǔ	now and then **g.** bù shí de		to work **o.** shàngbān
before work **d.** shàngbān qián	rarely **h.** hěn shǎo		in the restaurant **p.** zài fànguǎn
	always **i.** měi		at home **q.** zài jiā
	never **j.** cónglái bù		

Put it together   Shàngbān qián, wǒ xué Zhōngwén. Wǒ měitiān kāichē qù shàngbān. Wǒ zài jiā zhǔnbèi wǔfàn. Wǒ hěn shǎo zài fànguǎn chī wǔfàn. Wǒ huí jiā yǐhòu zuò wǎnfàn. Wǎnfàn yǐhòu, wǒ kàn diànshì. (Before work, I study Chinese. Everyday, I drive to work. I prepare my lunch at home. I rarely eat lunch at a restaurant. When I return home, I make dinner. After dinner, I watch TV.)

Your turn: use the hack   Students' answers may vary. Here are some example answers.
1 a. Wǒmen yìqǐ zài fànguǎn. Wǒ hěn gāoxìng. / Wǒmen yìqǐ lái de. Wǒmen zài fànguǎn. Wǒ hěn gāoxìng. **b.** Wǒ yào qù cānguān Gùgōng. Wǒ yào nǐ gēn wǒ qù. **c.** Wǒ xiànzài bù xiǎng qù chāoshì. Wǒ xiǎng xiàwu zài qù. **2 a.** shuō; Zhōngguó; hěn yǒuyìsi **b.** Xué; Zài; kāishǐ

Put it together   **1** Lái Jiāhōu yǐhòu, nǐ xiàn xūyào qù hǎibiān. Nǐ yě yīnggāi qù Hǎoláiwù rúguǒ nǐ yǒu shíjiān. Yǒu hěnduō hǎokàn de dìfang. (When you come to California, you need to go to the beach first. You should also go to Hollywood if you have time. There are a lot of nice places to see.) **2** Zhè ge zhōumò wǒ bù tài máng. Wǒ kěyǐ xīngqīliù qù. Wǒmen yīnggāi zài nǎli jiànmiàn? Shénme shíhou kāishǐ? Shénme shíhou zuò wán? Wǒ xūyào shénme? Wǒ jué de huì hěn yǒuqù! (This weekend I'm not too busy. I can go Saturday. Where should we meet? What time does it start? When will we be done? What do I need? I think it will be fun!)

COMPLETING UNIT 8

Check your understanding   **1** Wǒ měitiān shàngbān. Shàngbān qián wǒ chī zǎofàn. Wǒ yě hē kāfēi. Zài zhōngwǔ, wǒ gēn wǒ de tóngshì qù fànguǎn chī wǔfàn. Huíjiā yǐhòu, wǒ gēn jiārén yìqǐ chī wǎnfàn. Wǎnfàn chī wán yǐhòu, wǒ hé wǒ érzi kàn yì běn shū. (I go to work everyday. Before I go to work, I eat breakfast. I also

drink coffee. In the afternoon, I go to lunch at a restaurant with my coworkers. When I return home, I eat dinner with my family. When dinner is finished, I read a book with my son.) **2 a** měitiān **b** kāfēi **c** tā de tóngshì **d** wǎnfàn **e** kàn yì běn shū

MISSION SCRIPT – MODEL

Wǒ xīngqīyī shàngxué. Wǒ qí zìxíngchē qù xuéxiào. Wǒ xīngqī'èr hé xīngqīsì yě shàngxué. Wǒ xīngqīsān gōngzuò. Wǒ měi ge zhōumò yě gōngzuò. Xīngqīwǔ wǎnshàng, wǒ gēn wǒ de fùmǔ chī wǎnfàn. Wǒ xīwàng yǒu yìtiān néng gēn fùmǔ yìqǐ qù nà ge xīn de Zhōngguó fànguǎn chī wǎnfàn. Xiànzài wǒ tài máng. Wǒ bù néng qù. (I go to school on Monday. I ride my bike to school. I also go to school on Tuesday and Thursday. I work on Wednesday. I also work every weekend. Friday night, I eat dinner with my parents. One day, I would like to go to the new Chinese restaurant with my parents to eat dinner. I'm too busy now. I am not able to go.)

UNIT 9

CONVERSATION 1

Wǒ hěn kuài jiùyào huí Zhījiāgě le.

Figure it out   **1 a.** It's Lucy's last week, not her last day. (yì zhōu) **b.** Lucy should buy her parents some gifts, not books. (lǐwù) **c.** Nanluoguxiang is a very famous hutong, not Shanghai. **d.** They're planning to take a walk around Houhai after they go to Nanluoguxiang. (yǐhòu) **2 a.** last week **b.** That's too bad. **c.** Then ... **3 a.** hěn kuài / zài yí ge xīngqī **b.** jiāoqū de fēnwéi **c.** hǎo **d.** lǐwù **e.** bù zhīdao; xiǎng sànbù **f.** kěyǐ zhǎo ge dìfang mǎi bīngqílín **4 a.** Xiǎng jiā ma? **b.** zhù zài jiāoqū **c.** fēicháng yǒuhǎo **d.** Wǒ ài gòuwù. **e.** nà yào kàn

Notice **1** a. Xiǎng jiā ma? / Wǒ yě xiǎng nǐ
b. wǒ huí qù / Wǒ hěn kuài huíqù **c.** Wǒ
xiǎngshòu / Wǒ zhēn xiǎngshòu zhù zài Běijīng
d. ránhòu wǒmen lèi le / Ránhòu wǒmen lèi le
kěyǐ xiūxí **2** a. 1 **b.** 4 **c.** 3 **d.** 2 **3** a. jiāoqū
b. mountain **c.** tree(s) **d.** tàiyáng **e.** yínháng
f. jǐngjú **g.** shìzhèng tīng **h.** pharmacy / drug store
i. tǐyùchǎng **j.** túshūguǎn

Practice **1** Students' answers vary.
2 Students' answers vary. Example: Wǒ zhù zài
yí ge gōngyù. Wǒ zhù zài dì jiǔ lóu. Fùjìn yǒu yí
ge dà gōngyuán. Wǒ xǐhuān zài zhè ge gōngyuán
sànbù. (I live in an apartment. I live on the ninth
floor. Very near, there's a big park. I like to go
to this park to walk/stroll around.) **3** Student's
answers vary. Example: Wǒ de fùmǔ zhù zài
yì suǒ dà fángzi. Tāmen zài hòuyuàn yǒu yí ge
yóuyǒngchí. Zài jiēshang, yǒu yì jiā fāngbiàn de
chāoshì. Nàli yǒu hěnduō hǎochī de dōngxi. (My
parents live in a big house. They have a pool
in the backyard. On the street, there is a very
convenient supermarket. There are a lot of tasty
things there.)

Vocab explanation **1** a.Tiānqì hǎo. **b.** Tiānqì
bù hǎo. Tài zāogāo le! **2** Students' answers vary.

Put it together Students' answers will vary.
Example answer: Wǒ zhù zài yí ge xiǎo chéngshì.
Bù yuǎn de dìfang, yǒu yí piàn xiǎo sēnlín hé yí
ge hú. Tiānqì chángcháng hěn liáng. Wǒ ài zài
sēnlín li sànbù. Yīnwèi wǒ de chéngshì hěn xiǎo,
zuǒyòu de línjū wǒ dōu rènshi. (I live in a small
city. Not far, there is a small forest and a lake.
The weather is very cool. I love to walk in the
forest. Because my city is small, I know about
everyone.)

Grammar explanation: separable words
1 a. chī guo fàn **b.** shuì guo jiào **c.** kāi guo huì
2 a. páipái duì **b.** qǐngqǐng jià **c.** pǎopǎo bù
3 a. kàn bu kànbìng **b.** liáo bu liáotiān **c.** chū bu
chūchāi

CONVERSATION 2

Lucy says her sister is hěn yǒnggǎn (very brave),
her brother is niánqīng (young), and her parents
are chuántǒng (traditional).

Figure it out **1** a. cuò **b.** duì **c.** cuò **2** a. chá
/ tángguǒ **b.** hěn yǒnggǎn **c.** wúliáo **d.** chuántǒng
de dōngxi **3** a. Zhè ràng wǒ xiǎng qǐ lái. **b.** Tā
zhēn xiǎng yào. **c.** jìniànpǐn **d.** zìjǐ **e.** chuántǒng
f. hěn wúliáo

Notice **1** a. yǒnggǎn (brave) **b.** niánqīng
(young) **c.** wúliáo (boring) **d.** piányi (cheap)
e. diànzǐ (electronic) **f.** chuántǒng (traditional)
2 a. róngyì / nán **b.** tèbié / diǎnxíng **c.** bèn /
cōngming **d.** xiàndài / chuántǒng **e.** yǒnggǎn /
hàixiū **f.** lǎo / niánqīng **3** a. hàixiū **b.** brave
c. chǒu **d.** piàoliang / měi **e.** tall **f.** fun / interesting
g. diǎnxíng **h.** bù yúkuài **i.** pessimistic **j.** lèguān
k. jiāo'ào **l.** modest **m.** hǎoxiào **n.** serious
o. stupid **p.** smart **q.** míngzhì **r.** average
s. yǒuhǎo **4** Students' answers will vary.

Put it together Students' answers will vary.
Example answers:

Wǒ de nán péngyou jiào Lándí. Tā shì jīnglǐ. Tā
hěn wàixiàng. Tā yě hěn yǒuqù. Tā bú tài gāo. Tā
hěn cōngming, hěn shuài. (My boyfriend's name
is Randy. He is a manager. He is outgoing. He is
also funny. He is not too tall. He is very smart,
very handsome.)

Wǒ māma shì lǐfàshī. Tā hěn piàoliang. Yǐqián
tā zǒngshì hěn máng, dànshì xiànzài tā yǒu
gèng duō shíjiān le. Tā bú hàixiū. (My mom is a
hairdresser. She is very pretty. Before she was
always very busy, but now she has more time.
She is not shy.)

Grammar explanation: the big one
1 a. rènzhēn de **b.** hóngsè de **c.** lǜsè de
d. zuìhǎo de **2** a. Hēisè de duōshao qián?

b. Wǒ xiànzài kěyǐ mǎi lǜsè de ma? **c.** Xìnyòngkǎ, kěyǐ ma? **d.** Piányi yìdiǎn. **3 a.** long **b.** short (for height) **c.** thin / slim

Put it together   Students' answers will vary. Example:

Wǒ kǒu kě. Wǒ xiǎng mǎi yì bēi yǐnliào. Wǒ yào sūdǎshuǐ. Tīngzhuāng … Hóngsè de. Zài Měiguó hěn liúxíng. (I'm thirsty. I would like to buy a drink. I want soda. The can … the red one. It's very popular in America.)

COMPLETING UNIT 9

Check your understanding   **1** zài gōngyuán **2** xiǎo **3** yǒu hěnduō rén **4** māma **5** gāoxìng **6** zhèngzài wán **7** bīngqílín **8** qiǎokèlì de

MISSION SCRIPT – MODEL

Wǒ zuì xǐhuān de chéngshì shì Bèi'ěrfǎsītè. Tā zài hǎiyáng fùjìn. Tā yǒu hěn cháng de lìshǐ. Dànshì tiānqì chángcháng hěn lěng. Zǒngshì xiàyǔ. Dànshì wǒ xǐhuān zhè zhǒng tiānqì. Fángzi hěn dà. Bèi'ěrfǎsītè rén hěn yǒuhǎo. (My favorite city is Belfast. It is near the ocean. It has a lot of history. But the weather is very cold. It's always raining.But I like this weather. House are big. Belfast people are friendly.)

UNIT 10

PUT YOUR CONVERSATION STRATEGIES INTO ACTION

Students' answers will vary. Examples:

1 Nǐ hǎo. **2** Wǒ jiào Benny. Wǒ yě hěn gāoxìng rènshi nǐ. **3** Wǒ xué Zhōngwén yīnwèi wǒ xiǎng zhù zài Zhōngguó. **4** Wǒ yě huì shuō Xībānyáyǔ, Pútáoyáyǔ hé Fǎyǔ. **5** Duìbùqǐ, wǒ bù míngbai. Nǐ kěyǐ xiě xiàlái ma?

COMPLETING UNIT 10

Check your understanding

⋯⟩ What is her name? Yǔyān
⋯⟩ Where is she from? Hā'ěrbīn
⋯⟩ Where does she live now? Xīyǎtú (Seattle)
⋯⟩ How long has she been teaching Chinese? liù nián
⋯⟩ Does she speak any other languages? If so, which ones? huì; Rìyǔ
⋯⟩ What are some of the things she is interested in? xǐhuān zuòfàn, dǎ pīngpāng qiú, hé chūqù sànbù

ACKNOWLEDGMENTS

Though my name and face may be on the cover, there are many people whose voices and ideas are in these pages.

I was fortunate to meet many native Mandarin speakers who encouraged me when I was a struggling beginner. I thank them for their patience. My Mandarin-learning experience has been filled with friends who made the language come alive and gave me the passion to inspire others.

There aren't enough praises I can sing about my editor **Sarah Cole**, who first reached out to me with the exciting prospect of collaborating with *Teach Yourself*. She worked with me over two years with unwavering support and passion for my vision of a modern language course. I cannot imagine that any other publisher could have brought so much life to these courses.

I am grateful to the rest of the *Teach Yourself* team in both the UK and US, who showed incredible enthusiasm in creating a totally new kind of language course and whose commitment has helped grow the series. In particular, I'd like to thank **Helen Rogers** and **Lisa Hutchins** for making sure the many pieces all came together perfectly.

This book benefitted greatly from the early involvement of **Judith Meyer** and **Joseph Lemien** whose great ideas helped to successfully apply my method to Mandarin and all of its complexities.

And lastly, this course would not exist without the mammoth efforts of **Shannon Kennedy**, who worked tirelessly to transform my original courses into Mandarin and, with the perspective of an experienced learner, has made *Language Hacking Mandarin* an effective and achievable course for beginner learners. **Dr. Licheng Gu** kindly bestowed upon this publication his vast experience and expertise as a professor of Mandarin for over 30 years at Princeton and Northwestern Universities. Dr. Gu ensured that the content of this course genuinely meets the needs of a modern language learner. I am honored to have him as my co-author and forever grateful for his contribution, which turned my good course into a great one.

Practice your missions and improve your speaking with a teacher online.

As a member of the **#languagehacking** community, new users can get $5 off any $10 italki credit purchase using the discount code "languagehacking" at checkout.

www.italki.com/languagehacking